UNEDUCATED GUESSES

UNEDUCATED GUESSES

Using Evidence to Uncover Misguided
Education Policies

❧ ❧

HOWARD WAINER

PRINCETON UNIVERSITY PRESS
PRINCETON AND OXFORD

Requests for permission to reproduce material from this work
should be sent to Permissions, Princeton University Press

Published by Princeton University Press, 41 William Street,
Princeton, New Jersey 08540

In the United Kingdom: Princeton University Press, 6 Oxford Street,
Woodstock, Oxfordshire OX20 1TW

press.princeton.edu

ISBN 978-0-691-14928-8

British Library Cataloging-in-Publication Data is available

Wainer, Howard.

Uneducated guesses: using evidence to uncover
misguided education policies / Howard Wainer.

p.   cm.

Includes bibliographical references and index.

ISBN 978-0-691-14928-8 (hardcover : alk. paper)   1. Universities
and colleges--United States--Entrance examinations.
2. Education—Standards   United States.   3. Educational evaluation—
United States.   I. Title.

LB2353.2.W35 2011

378.1'662--dc22

2010053097

This book has been composed in Palatino

Printed on acid-free paper.

Printed in the United States of America

1 3 5 7 9 10 8 6 4 2

To the parents of my childhood,
and the children of my parenthood.

For a successful technology, reality must
take precedence over public relations,
for nature cannot be fooled.
—Richard P. Feynman

Contents

Preface

I don't know whether it is the age we live in, or the age I have lived to, but whichever, I have lately found myself shouting at the TV screen disturbingly often. Part of the reason for this may be the unchecked growth of the crotchety side of my nature. But some of the blame for these untoward outbreaks can be traced directly to the remarkable dopiness that substitutes for wisdom in modern society.

Ideas whose worth diminishes with data and thought are too frequently offered as the only way to do things. Promulgators of these ideas either did not look for data to test their ideas, or worse, actively avoided considering evidence that might discredit them.

Ranting in the privacy of my own home spares me embarrassment, but alas does nothing the remediate the problem. So from time to time I would put pixel to screen and describe the proposal or policy that had aroused me along with empirical evidence that tests the idea. In a surprisingly short time I had collected enough of these excursions to provide a coherent story.

This book is that story.

It deals with education in general and the use of tests and test scores in support of educational goals in particular. My forty years of experience in this area has reduced the diffidence I ordinarily feel about offering opinions. But the opinions, and the work involved in finding and analyzing the data that supports them, was not accomplished alone. I had help. It is my pleasure now to offer my gratitude publicly.

First, to my employer, the National Board of Medical Examiners, which provided the time and resources to prepare this work. And more specifically to Don Melnick, the Board's president, Ron Nungester, senior vice president, and Brian Clauser, assistant vice president, who, in addition to resources, provided the encouragement and quietude to get it completed.

Next to coauthors who collaborated with me in the original work that is anthologized here. Specifically, Peter Baldwin, Henry Braun, Paul Holland, William Lichten, and David Thissen. I thank you all. Without you, this would not have been possible. In addition there were a number of people who have read and commented on various pieces in preliminary forms: Wayne Camara, Stephen Clyman, Monica Cuddy, John Durso, Sam Palmer, Peter Scoles, and Linda Steinberg.

Of course, throughout all that I have done over the past eight years is the shadow of Editha Chase, who has been my right hand. Her smiling face always accompanies the resolution of whatever problem I set before her. A heartfelt thank-you is surely too small, but alas is all that I have to give.

And finally, the staff of Princeton University Press, whose intelligence born of long experience, turned my raw manuscript into the finished product you now hold in your hand. And of course, Vickie Kearn, math editor at the Press and my friend. Her enthusiasm and support have always been, and remain now, very special to me.

⌒⌒

In September 2008 the National Association for College Admission Counseling (NACAC) published a report that made a number of recommendations for changes in the admissions process. Three of the major ones were (a) to make standard admissions exams optional, (b) to substitute specific achievement tests for the more general aptitude tests currently used, and (c) to replace the PSAT as a screening test for Merit Scholarships with a more vigorous screener without a fixed minimum eligibility score. In the first three chapters I use evidence to examine the value of each of these proposals. In the subsequent chapters I discuss how well evidence and logic supports (or doesn't) a number of other actions suggested or taken. Chapter 9 focuses on the use of student performance data to evaluate teachers. I am well aware of the current heated debates about the desirability of such an action. The challenges associated with accomplishing such an undertaking go well beyond dogma and involve subtle and important issues that are at the very heart of the validity of scientific inference.

What follows is an annotated table of contents. I have included these extended descriptions for two reasons:

a. To whet the appetite of the reader by providing more information about the contents of the chapter than could be accomplished in a short chapter title, and

b. To provide at least a summary of the contents for those too busy to read the whole chapter in hopes that it will increase their skepticism of the policy being discussed.

Chapter 1, "On the Value of Entrance Exams: What Happens When the SAT Is Made Optional?" Since 1969 colleges have begun to adopt an "SAT optional" policy for applicants. How has this policy affected the quality of entering classes? As luck would have it, essentially all applicants take the SAT, and then after receiving their scores decide whether or not to submit them. Through a special data-gathering effort we are able to compare the scores of those who submit them with those who decide not to. Not surprisingly, those who withhold their scores have done much worse. Paired with this, we also discover that their subsequent performance in college is about as much lower than the other students as would have been predicted from their lower SAT scores. However, by excluding lower-scoring students from the school's SAT average, the school's national rankings, which have mean SAT score as an important component, go up.

Chapter 2, "On Substituting Achievement Tests for Aptitude Tests in College Admissions." This notion is one that only makes sense if you say it fast. Test scores are used by admissions officers to make comparisons among applicants. The idea of substituting specific achievement tests for more general aptitude tests has, as its basis, the idea that students will then be able to show off expertise directly in the content areas of their special competence. But then how are comparisons to be made? Is your French better than my physics? Was Babe Ruth a better hitter than Mozart was a composer? In this chapter I discuss the too often arcane, but, alas, critical, area of test equating, in which scores on different tests are made comparable, including the limits of the technology.

Chapter 3, "On Rigid Decision Rules for Scholarships." Having hard and fast cutoffs has always been a tough sell. How can we say that someone who scores just above the cutoff is okay and someone just below is not? Surely our educational measuring instruments are not up to such precise decision-making. In this chapter I begin with the wise strategy adopted for the use of the nineteenth-century civil service exams in India, and show why the current approach is a far fairer solution to a difficult problem than the alternative recommended by NACAC.

Chapter 4, "The Aptitude-Achievement Connection: Using an Aptitude Test to Aid in Allocating Educational Resources." Over the last decade there has been an enormous increase in the number of advanced placement courses offered in high schools, in the number of high schools that offer them, and the number of students who enroll in them. In the face of scarce resources and low performance of students on national assessments, is this a sensible development? In this chapter I describe an analytic tool that predicts how well students will do on Advanced Placement exams and argue that using it would allow the wiser allocation of resources.

Chapter 5, "Comparing the Incomparable: On the Importance of Big Assumptions and Scant Evidence." There is no limit to the distances some will go to in order to make invidious comparisons. In this chapter I discuss how international comparisons are made and why the validity of such comparisons rests on assumptions that are both shaky and untestable. I illustrate this argument with examples from the United States, Canada, and Israel.

Chapter 6, "On Examinee Choice in Educational Testing." Modern multiple-choice tests have been criticized for not providing an authentic context for measurement. The critics prefer test formats that feature essays and other kinds of extended response questions. A difficulty with this approach arises in real-world situations because of limited testing time. One cannot ask examinees to answer a large number of essay questions. But if only a very small number of questions are asked, the possibility increases that an unfortunate choice of topics by the test developer may disadvantage some examinees. This has been ameliorated by allowing examinees to choose from among several essay topics. In this chapter I show that this strategy fails empirically, exacerbating intergroup differences and disadvantaging women.

Chapter 7, "What If Choice Is Part of the Test?" Suppose we consider the choice of which item to answer as part of the test. We can sensibly do this if the skills related to choosing wisely are well established and agreed by all participants to be a legitimate part of the curriculum that is being tested and that all options available could, plausibly, be asked of each examinee. If this is all true, it leads to a remarkable and surprising result—we can offer choice on a test and obtain satisfactory results without grading the answers! In fact, the examinees don't even have to write an answer; it is enough that they merely indicate their preferences. In this chapter I demonstrate how this works out.

Chapter 8, "A Little Ignorance Is a Dangerous Thing: How Statistics Rescued a Damsel in Distress." Whenever a testing organization makes a mistake—for example, an item that was misscored or some test answer sheets that were misread—we read about it in the paper. Yet the most grievous errors that take place in educational testing are perpetuated by the users of the test scores. In this chapter I describe how a third-grade teacher was suspended because her class did better than a superficial analysis of the scores on a statewide exam indicated was likely. It was concluded that the class performance reflected cheating. A subsequent, more careful analysis of the data indicated that the class's performance was in line with expectations. When these analyses were laid out in a court hearing, she was exonerated.

Chapter 9, "Assessing Teachers from Student Scores: On the Practicality of Value-Added Models." Powerful forces are currently arrayed in support of the assessment of teachers using the gains demonstrated by their students' scores on exams given at the beginning and end of the school year. In this chapter I discuss the epistemological and practical problems with this approach.

Chapter 10, "Shopping for Colleges When What We Know Ain't." We often hear that after our house, our car is the largest purchase we will make. In line with this claim, we are bombarded with information to help us make an informed decision. Yet as anyone who has recently paid the college tab for one or more children well understands, those expenses dwarf cars, and indeed three children at a private college can easily surpass the cost of the family house. Yet the advice we get about choosing colleges is remarkably short on hard evidence. In this chapter

I evaluate a new approach to ranking colleges, and conclude that it falls far short of what is required.

Chapter 11, "Of CATs and Claims: The First Step toward Wisdom." When we change the format in which tests are administered we must also change some of the rules. In this chapter examine what went wrong when attempts were made to continue to use rules devised for traditional paper and pencil tests when the tests were administered intelligently by computer. Along the way, we find that misunderstanding increases when the distinctions between data and evidence are blurred.

UNEDUCATED GUESSES

Introduction

It is rare to know exactly when and where an idea originates. But for me it was Monday, September 7, 1970, at 5:45 P.M. I was on the South Side of Chicago walking north on Dorchester Avenue, between Fifty-sixth and Fifty-seventh streets. I was a new assistant professor at the University of Chicago, and was walking home from my first day of work. Standing in the street was a very large, black motorcycle next to an even larger, fearsome looking, man. He was wearing motorcycle boots and a leather jacket, had long hair and a full beard, and was speaking with a young woman whose apartment was in a building two doors down from mine. In passing I overheard a snippet of conversation. He shook his head in response to something she said and replied, "But that's an epistemological question."

Epistemology was almost a foreign word and concept to me at that time. I had heard the term before. Adjoined to metaphysics and phenomenology, it formed an almost holy triumvirate in the requisite undergraduate introductory course in philosophy, but it had made no impact. However, hearing it used on the street made a difference. Returning home, I looked it up and found "method for gaining knowledge," which might translate into "scientific method," which might then be specialized to "procedures used by actual practicing scientists."

The iconic physicist Richard Feymann provided, as only he could, a clear description of modern epistemology in his famous Messenger Lectures, given at Cornell in 1964 (subsequently anthologized in his book *The Character of Physical Law*):

In general we look for a new law by the following process. First we guess it. Then we compute the consequences of the guess to see what would be implied if this law that we guessed is right. Then we compare the result of the computation to nature, with experiment or experience, compare it directly with observation, to see if it works. If it disagrees with experiment it is wrong. In that simple statement is the key to science.

It does not make any difference how beautiful your guess is. It does not make any difference how smart you are, who made the guess, or what his name is—if it disagrees with experiment it is wrong. That is all there is to it. (1965, 156)

I don't know what epistemological question was being discussed on Dorchester Avenue forty years ago, but two key ones are how and when evidence should be used. It was clear that Feynman placed evidence in an exalted position. It vetoed all else. Yet strangely, at least to me, this point of view is not universal.

We hear the term *evidenced-based decision making* in many fields; medicine, education, economics, and political policy, to pick four. Its frequent use implies that this is a new and modern way to try to solve modern problems. If what we are doing now is evidence based, what were we doing previously?[1]

How can we consider the use of evidence in science new? Hasn't evidence been at the very core of science for millennia? The short answer is no. Making decisions evidence-based has always been a tough row to hoe, for once you commit to it, no idea, no matter how beautiful, no matter how desirable, can withstand an established contrary fact, regardless of how ugly that fact might be. The conflict between evidence and faith in the modern world is all around us, even in scientific issues for which faith is not required.[2] So it is not surprising that using evidence to make decisions is taking a long time to catch on. The origination of the formal idea of using evidence as a method for gaining knowledge is often dated, as are so many things, with Aristotle (384 B.C.–322 B.C.) but its pathway thereafter was not smooth, for once one commits to using

---

[1] When I suggested that evidence-based medicine's predecessor must have been faith-based, my boss, Donald Melnick, corrected me and said that he liked to think that medicine was intelligently designed.

[2] A story is told of a conversation between Napoleon and Laplace in which Napoleon congratulated Laplace on the publication of his masterwork, *Traité de Mécanique Céleste*, but then added that he was disappointed because "no where in this great work was the name of God mentioned even once." Laplace is said to have responded, "I did not need that hypothesis."

evidence to make decisions, facts take precedence over opinion.[3] And not all supporters of an empirical approach had Alexander the Great to watch their backs. Hence it took almost 2000 years before Francis Bacon (1561–1626) repopularized the formal use of evidence, an approach that was subsequently expanded and amplified by British empiricists: the Englishman John Locke (1632–1704), the Irishman George Berkeley (1685–1753), and the Scot David Hume (1711–1776).

Although the development of a firm philosophic basis for incorporating evidence in how we know things was necessary, it was not sufficient. Much more was required. Part of what was needed was a deep understanding of uncertainty. This was recognized and, almost coinciding with the onset of the twentieth century, began the development of statistics, the Science of Uncertainty. Statistics' beginning was primarily mathematical, with a focus on fitting equations to data and making judgments about the legitimacy of the inferences one might draw from them. This changed in 1977 with the publication of John Tukey's (1915–2000) *Exploratory Data Analysis*. Tukey, a towering figure of twentieth-century science, legitimized the practice of the atheoretical plotting of points with the goal of finding suggestive patterns. He pointed out that "the greatest value of a graph is when it *forces* us to see what we never expected." Tukey's key contribution was his legitimization of this sort of empirical epistemology. He likened exploratory analysis to detective work, in which the scientist gathers evidence and generates hypotheses, the guesses that Feyman referred to.

Traditional statistical methods were more judicial in nature, in which the evidence was weighed and a decision was made. The modern scientific world has both the philosophic and mechanical tools to use evidence to generate hypotheses and to test them. Yet the rigorous thinking that the scientific method requires has yet to penetrate public discourse fully. Guesses are made, sometimes from intuition, sometimes from hope, sometimes from dogma. But too often these guesses only make sense if you say them fast—for when they are tested with evidence and logic, they are found faulty.

[3] Bertrand Russell reports that even Aristotle had trouble following the tenets of empiricism in all aspects of his own life, for he maintained that women have fewer teeth than men; although he was twice married, it never occurred to him to verify this statement by examining his wives' mouths.

In the chapters to follow I will show that if we decide to use evidence, we can discover things. Usually these discoveries add to our store of knowledge, and we are happy to have found them. But sometimes what we discover conflicts sharply with our intuition. It is in situations like these that our commitment to empiricism, as a way of knowing things, gets tested. When this experience of contradictory evidence happens—to return to the sidewalk wisdom with which I began this introduction—what we decide to do becomes an epistemological question.

Evidence of success in contemporary education encompasses many things, but principal among them are test scores. When scores are high, we congratulate all involved. When they are low, we look to make changes. When there are differences between groups, ethnic or gender, we are concerned. If these differences shrink we are pleased; if they grow larger we often metaphorically shoot either the messenger (the test) or the educators.

Shooting the messenger as a strategy for dealing with bad news has a long history. And it persists despite its low likelihood of sustainable success. In this book I discuss the use of tests and their associated scores as evidence in making educational decisions. The examples chosen illustrate only a small portion of the range of uses to which tests are put—from traditional uses like making the triage decision about admittance to college (chapters 1 and 2), to awarding scholarships (chapter 3), to allocating educational resources for instruction (chapter 4), to judging the quality of instruction (chapter 9). In the course of these illustrations it seems worthwhile to illuminate some commonsense ideas on the use of tests that, with some thought, we discover are deeply flawed (chapters 5, 6, 7, and 8).

Let us start at the beginning.

The use of mental tests appears to be almost as ancient as civilization itself. The Bible (Judges 12:4–6) provides an early reference in Western culture. It describes a short verbal test that the Gileadites used to uncover the fleeing Ephraimites hiding in their midst. The test was one item long. Candidates had to pronounce the word *shibboleth*; Ephraimites apparently pronounced the initial *sh* as *s*. The consequences of failure were severe, as the Bible records that the banks of the Jordon River were littered with 42,000 bodies of Ephraimites (it is unknown how many of those 42,000 were Gileadites with a lisp).

There is substantial evidence of the beginnings of an extensive testing program in China at around 2200 B.C., predating the biblical

Jephthah then called together the men of Gilead and fought against Ephraim. The Gileadites struck them down because the Ephraimites had said, "You Gileadites are renegades from Ephraim and Manasseh."

The Gileadites captured the fords of the Jordan leading to Ephraim, and whenever a survivor of Ephraim said, "Let me cross over," the men of Gilead asked him, "Are you an Ephraimite?" If he replied, "No," they said, "All right, say 'Shibboleth.'" If he said, "Sibboleth," because he could not pronounce the word correctly, they seized him and killed him at the fords of the Jordan.

Forty-two thousand Ephraimites were killed at that time.

Judges 12:4–6

program by almost a thousand years. The emperor of China is said to have examined his officials every third year. This set a precedent for periodic exams in China that was to persist for a very long time. In 1115 B.C., at the beginning of the Shang dynasty, formal testing procedures were instituted for candidates for office.

The Chinese discovered the fundamental tenet of testing:

a relatively small sample of an individual's performance, measured under carefully controlled conditions, could yield an accurate picture of that individual's ability to perform under much broader conditions for a longer period of time.

China's testing program, augmented and modified, has lasted almost uninterrupted for more than four thousand years. It was advocated by Voltaire and Quesnay for use in France, where it was adopted in 1791, only to be (temporarily) abolished by Napoleon. It was cited by British reformers in 1833 as their model for selecting trainees into the Indian civil service system—the precursor of the British civil service. The success of the British system influenced Senator Charles Sumner and Representative Thomas Jenckes in their development of the American civil service examination system that they introduced into Congress in 1868. There was a careful description of the British and Chinese systems in Jenckes's report *Civil Service of the United States,* which laid the foundation for the establishment of the Civil Service Act passed in January 1883.

The use of large-scale testing grew exponentially in the United States after World War I, when it was demonstrated that a mass-administered version of what was essentially an IQ test (what was then called "Army Alpha") improved the accuracy and efficiency of the placement of recruits into the various military training programs. The precursors of what would eventually become the SAT were modeled on Army Alpha.

Testing has prospered over the four millennia of its existence because it offers a distinct improvement over the method that had preceded it.

> *To count is modern practice, the ancient method was to guess.*
>
> —Samuel Johnson

Testing also fit comfortably into the twentieth-century meritocratic zeitgeist where advancement was based increasingly on what you knew and could do instead of your lineage and wealth.

But as time has passed and test usage increased, the demands that we have made on test scores have increased, as have the "fineness" of the distinctions we wish to make. As this has happened, tests and how they are scored have improved. These improvements have occurred for three principal reasons:

1. The demands made on the test scores have become more strenuous.
2. We have gathered more and more evidence about how well various alternatives perform.
3. Our eyes have become accustomed to the dim light in those often dark and Byzantine alleys where tests and psychometrics live.

But although deep knowledge of testing has increased, testing's usage has expanded well beyond the cadre of experts who understand it. In the modern world, too often those who use test scores as evidence to guide their decisions are unacquainted with testing's strengths and weaknesses. Instead they often find that test scores are (to borrow Al Gore's evocative phrase) an inconvenient truth. In short they are facts that get in the way of the story that they want to believe. When this happens, either the facts are ignored or their accuracy is maligned. In this section I will lay out some facts and arguments in the hope that future decision-makers will understand better how to use this marvelous invention to assess the state of the educational enterprise and thence to amend its flaws.

The first three examples all grow from a report published in September 2008 by the National Association for College Admission Counseling (NACAC). The report was critical of the current, widely used, college admissions exams, the SAT and the ACT, and made a number of recommendations for changes in the admissions process. It was reasonably wide-ranging and drew many conclusions while offering alternatives. A description of this report's findings was carried broadly in the media. Although well-meaning, many of the suggestions only make sense if you say them very fast.

Three of its major conclusions were the following:

1. Schools should consider making their admissions "SAT optional," that is allowing applicants to submit their SAT/ACT scores if they wish, but they should not be mandatory. The commission cites the success that pioneering schools with this policy have had in the past as proof of concept.
2. Schools should consider eliminating the SAT/ACT altogether and substituting achievement tests. The report cites the unfair effect of coaching as the motivation for this proposal. Its authors were not naive enough to suggest that because there was no coaching for achievement tests now that, if they carried higher stakes, coaching for them would not be offered. Rather they claimed that such coaching would be directly related to schooling and hence more beneficial to education than coaching that focused solely on test-taking skills.
3. The use of the PSAT with a rigid qualification cut-score for such scholarship programs as the Merit Scholarships should be immediately halted. It should be replaced with a more rigorous screening test without a fixed minimum eligibility score.

I use evidence to examine the validity of these recommendations in the first three chapters. This information provides enough momentum to carry us through the next seven chapters, in which we investigate other uses of tests within the educational system and discuss how they have been misused, as well as what can be done to ameliorate these problems.

1

◔◔ ◔◔

On the Value of Entrance Exams

What Happens When the SAT Is Made Optional?

On my shelf is a well-used copy of James Thurber's (1939) *Fables for Our Time*. In it is the fable of "The Glass in the Field." It seems that a builder had "left a huge square of plate glass standing upright in a field one day." Flying at high speed, a goldfinch struck the glass and later told a seagull, a hawk, an eagle, and a swallow about his injuries caused by the crystallized air. The gull, the hawk, and the eagle laughed and bet the goldfinch a dozen worms that they could fly the same route without encountering crystallized air, but the swallow declined to bet and was alone in escaping injury. Thurber's moral: "He who hesitates is sometimes saved." The point of this message is unhappily familiar to those who bought Edsels, Betamax video recorders, and, more recently, Hummers and Lehman Brothers stock.

Over the past two decades there has been extensive debate over the value that such admissions tests as the SAT and the ACT offer in improving the quality of college admissions decisions. This discussion has intensified with a recent announcement by William R. Fitzsimmons, the dean of admissions and financial aid at Harvard, as well as the chair of NACAC's Commission on Admissions.[1] The key recommendation was summed up in the *New York Times*' headline, which blared, "College Panel Urges Shift Away From SATs."

This chapter developed from H. Wainer, "What Happens If You Don't Require the SAT? Bowdoin College as an Example," The College Board, New York, February 1, 2006.
[1] *New York Times*, September 22, 2008, A14.

The commission's other conclusions were all related to the use and misuse of the well-known college admissions examinations, the SAT and ACT. It believed that colleges and universities ought to reconsider requiring these exams from their applicants. The commission concluded that for many schools such testing did more harm than good. It is at this moment that I join Thurber in pointing out that there is safety in caution. Before any decision of this magnitude is made, it is worthwhile to consider the consequences of such an action.

I feel about empirical evidence what Satchel Paige once said about money: It may not buy happiness, but it sure does steady the nerves. Fortunately for those who agree with my sentiments, there is evidence that can be examined about the consequences of eliminating the SAT. Let us begin such an examination with Bowdoin College.

Bowdoin College is a small, selective, liberal arts college located in Brunswick, Maine. Bowdoin eliminated the requirement of the SAT for its applicants in 1969, although if a student chooses to submit such scores, they are used in making the admissions decision. In the forty years since this policy was implemented, between 70 percent and 84 percent of Bowdoin's applicant pool each year has submitted SAT scores, and moreover, about the same proportion of those who submit SAT scores each year eventually attend Bowdoin. However, and of special importance to this inquiry, essentially all of those students who eventually attend Bowdoin actually take the SAT.[2]

A naive look at the performance of Bowdoin's students on the SAT might begin with a comparison of the average scores obtained by those students in comparison with other schools of similar average performance. Such data are shown in table 1.1. We see that Bowdoin places second, just behind Northwestern, but that the range of mean

---

[2] The results I report here are based on data gathered by the Admitted Class Evaluation Service (ACES) and collected as part of the joint ETS and College Board New Capabilities Research project. I am grateful for their permission to use these data to help illuminate this issue. Of course, they should not be held responsible for the conclusions I have drawn. Also I would like to thank Karen Castellano for some of the analyses reported here. These results were originally made public in a lecture held at The College Board on February 1, 2006, and were posted on the web in February 5, 2009, at http://blog .criteriacorp.com/2009/02/05dont-ask-dont-tell-the-new-rules-of-the-sat-and-college -admissions/. My gratitude to the College Board, and more specifically, to the College Board's Vice President Wayne Camara, for permitting these results to be posted and thus made available to use.

TABLE 1.1
Six Colleges and Universities with Similar Observed
Mean SAT Scores for the Entering Class of 1999

	All students	Submitted SAT scores		Did not submit
Institution	N	N	*Mean*	N
Northwestern University	1,654	1,505	1347	149
Bowdoin College	**379**	**273**	**1323**	**106**
Carnegie Mellon University	1,132	1,039	1319	93
Barnard College	419	399	1297	20
Georgia Institute of Technology	1,667	1,498	1294	169
Colby College	463	403	1286	60
MEANS AND TOTALS	**5,714**	**5,117**	**1316**	**597**

performance for these six institutions is sixty-one points. The difference between Bowdoin and Colby is mildly surprising, since they are very similar schools. We also note that Bowdoin has, by far, the largest proportion of attendees who did not submit SAT scores. This is not a surprise given that Bowdoin is alone in this group in not requiring the SAT for admission. The nonsubmitters at the other schools sent in ACT scores instead. I shall expand on this distinction later.

Why did the 106 Bowdoin students who did not submit SAT scores decide that this was a sensible strategy? We cannot know for sure, but two explanations seem plausible: (1) They knew that the SAT wasn't required and so decided "Why bother?" (2) They believed they would compare unfavorably with other applicants on the SAT and decided that submitting their scores would not help their cause.

Ordinarily the investigation would have to end here, because we cannot know which of these two plausible reasons is true. But we would have some supporting evidence if we knew how well those students who chose not to submit their SAT scores did on the SAT. It turns out that all 106 Bowdoin students who chose not to submit their SAT scores did, in fact, take the SAT. And through a special data-gathering effort at the Educational Testing Service supported by the College Board, those

Those students who don't submit SAT scores to Bowdoin score about120 points lower than those who do submit their scores

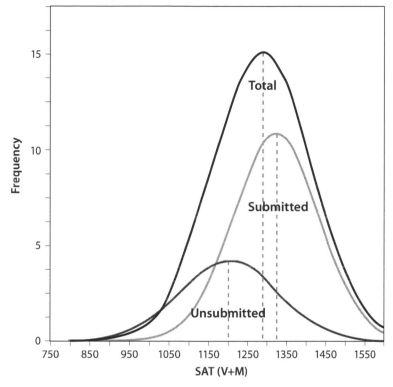

Figure 1.1. Normal approximation to the distributions of SAT scores among all members of the Bowdoin class of 1999

The curves drawn are not the actual distributions. What is shown in figure 1.1 is a normal approximation to Bowdoin students' actual distribution of SAT performance. In the rest of this discussion I shall continue to use this sort of normal approximation, but to justify this simplification let me illustrate what the actual distributions look like for these two groups. These are shown in figure 1.2. Comparing the results in figures 1.1 and 1.2 we find that the normal approximation is not an unreasonable characterization of what is actually happening. There are two aspects of the distributions that are missed in the approximation. The first is the small lump at about a score of 1000 that probably represents students who were accepted because of some unusual circumstance—perhaps because of their skill at a sport or because they were children of alumni or were members of an underrepresented group. The second is the overabundance of very high scores in the approximation that do not appear in the actual distribution. Despite these two shortcomings, a normal approximation is accurate enough in its general structure to provide a useful summary.

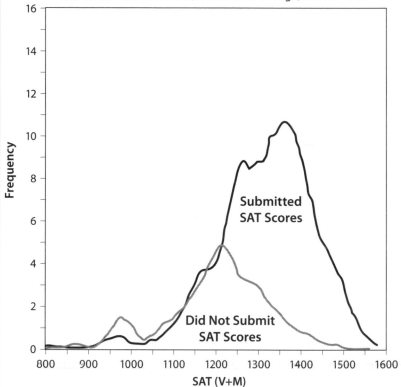

Figure 1.2. The distributions of SAT scores among all members of the Bowdoin class of 1999

scores were retrieved. Without peeking ahead, it seems plausible that those students who scored very well would probably submit them. Thus we ought to suspect that those who did not submit their scores did worse, on average, than those who did.

Thus it is no surprise that they did indeed do worse, a lot worse, at least on average. In figure 1.1 we see the distribution of SAT scores for all students in the Bowdoin class of 1999, in which 72 percent (273) of the class submitted scores to the college, while the remaining 28 percent (106) withheld them. The mean score of those who submitted them was 1323, while the mean score of those who did not was 1201, 122 points lower.

The evidence provided by the SAT scores from those students who did not submit them suggests that these students were wise in their decision. But because of lack of data on those students that did not matriculate at Bowdoin, we do not know how the bulk of those students with scores in this range fared in their application process.

How Well Did These Students Do in Their Studies at Bowdoin?

With these results in hand it makes sense to move on to the next logical question: How well did these students do in their studies at Bowdoin? Because the SAT is moderately predictive[3] of future performance in college, we might first predict that those students who did not submit their SAT scores, because they scored lower on the SAT than those students who did submit their scores, would also perform less well in their first-year courses. But because Bowdoin admitted them, ostensibly on the basis of their outstanding high school records, perhaps some sort of compensation took place and they did as well as the other students in their first-year courses?

The answer to this question is shown graphically in the score distributions in figure 1.3. We see that the students who did not submit their SAT scores not only did about 120 points worse on the SAT but also

[3] In most schools the SAT predicts performance in first-year courses about as well as four years of high school grades (Willingham 1985; Willingham et al. 1990), although this varies with trends over the decades of the 1970s and 1980s showing a slight increase in validity of the SAT and a slight decline in validity of high school grades.

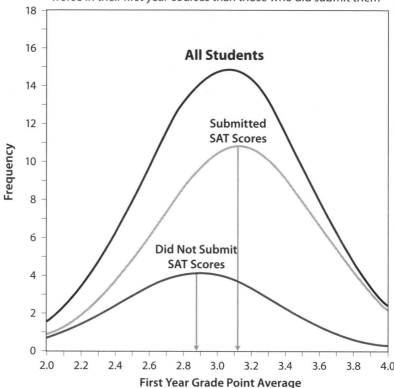

Figure 1.3. Normal approximation of the distributions of first-year grade point averages at Bowdoin shown as a function of whether or not applicants chose to submit their SAT scores

received grades 0.2 grade points (on a four-point scale) worse in their first-year courses.

This brief examination of one year of one school's experience in not requiring the SAT teaches us two things:

1. Students who choose not to submit SAT scores behave, on average, sensibly, for, again on average, they perform worse on the SAT than the students who do opt to submit their scores.
2. That whatever other variables are taken into account in the admission of applicants without SAT scores, they do not, on average, compensate for the lower performance on the SAT, for

students with lower SAT scores perform predictably worse in their first-year courses at Bowdoin.

Obviously, these conclusions are limited by the use of data from just one school and of just one year, but they are suggestive. Interpretation of these conclusions would be aided if we could put them into a broader context. To do this I looked at five other schools whose average SAT scores, of those members of the entering class of 1999 who chose to submit them, are close to Bowdoin's. These five schools all require an entrance exam, but will accept the ACT as a substitute for the SAT. And, indeed, a small percentage of their matriculating students submitted ACT scores instead of SAT scores (although virtually all of them took the SAT as well). The admissions committee typically converts the ACT score to an SAT scale and then treats all students in a coherent way.[4] These five schools, and some of their associated statistics, are shown in table 1.2. In that table we see that all of the observed mean SAT[5] scores at these institutions were within about thirty points of the overall mean of 1316; and that Bowdoin is second from the top of this elite group with a mean score of 1323. We also saw that except for Bowdoin about 90 percent of all students at these institutions submit SAT scores. The students who did not choose to submit SAT scores at these five other institutions submitted ACT scores instead. However they all took the SAT, and the scores they obtained are shown in table 1.2. At Bowdoin, the "nonsubmitters" had the lowest mean score of any school. This is likely to be a selection effect, although it is uncertain whether it is because students who had lower scores chose to apply to Bowdoin because of its policy of not requiring admission test scores, or because

---

[4] These data contain a mystery. Why do students who submit ACT scores at these schools do consistently worse on the SAT than those who submit SAT scores? There are three plausible explanations: (1) Students who submit ACT scores are consistently poorer students than those who submit SAT scores, (2) the conversion formula between ACT and SAT scores used by college admissions is inaccurate, or (3) those students who took both know the conversion formula and chose the score that puts them in the most favorable light, and hence capitalize on chance variations in score. The consistency across all schools of such students scoring lower on the SAT than the other students, and also performing worse in their first-year courses, provides compelling evidence that this is not some sort of statistical anomaly.

[5] Whenever I use the abbreviation *SAT score* I mean the sum of the scores for the verbal and the mathematical portions of the test; this is often abbreviated "SAT (V+M)."

TABLE 1.2
Summary of SAT Performance (Verbal + Math Scores) from Six
institutions of Similar SAT Performance among Those
Matriculating Students Who Submitted SAT Scores

Institution	All Students		Submitted SATs		Did Not Submit	
	N	Mean	N	Mean	N	Mean
Northwestern University	1,654	1338	1,505	1347	149	1250
Bowdoin College	**379**	**1288**	**273**	**1323**	**106**	**1201**
Carnegie Mellon University	1,132	1312	1,039	1319	93	1242
Barnard College	419	1293	399	1297	20	1213
Georgia Institute of Technology	1,667	1288	1,498	1294	169	1241
Colby College	463	1278	403	1286	60	1226
MEANS AND TOTALS	**5,714**	**1307**	**5,117**	**1316**	**597**	**1234**

Bowdoin had a greater likelihood of accepting such students than these other schools.

Note further that Bowdoin's rank of 2 on the basis of the observed SAT scores of the enrolled students drops to a tie for fifth (with Georgia Tech) if the entire class is used for comparison. Of course in most situations the only data that are observed are what have been submitted (the shaded portion of table 1.2) and so the shift in the placement of Bowdoin from second to fifth is invisible. Note also that the relative ordering of the other institutions, all of which require admissions tests and have a much smaller proportion of students who do not submit SAT scores, remains the same for the entire student body as it does for the observed portion. It has not escaped my attention nor, I suspect, that of some college administrators, that making the SATs optional means the SAT scores of the students who submit them will be higher than the scores of the entire student body. This allows the school to game the *US News and World Report* rankings, which use mean SAT score as a component of the ranking system. I don't believe that this tactic was Bowdoin's motivation, since it adopted this policy long before colleges were ranked according to SAT scores. But suspicions fall more heavily on recent adopters of optional SAT policies.

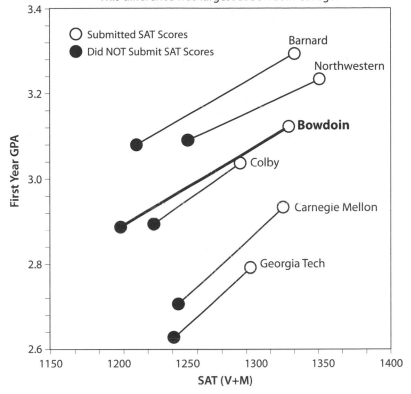

At all schools studied, students who submitted SAT scores performed better on BOTH the SAT and in their first year courses. This difference was largest at Bowdoin College.

Figure 1.4. The mean SAT coupled with the mean first-year GPA for the class of 1999 at six schools shown for those who submitted SAT scores for admission and those who did not

HOW IS BOWDOIN DIFFERENT FROM ALL OTHER SCHOOLS?

For purposes of completeness it makes sense to examine the performance of Bowdoin's students on both the SAT and first-year grades in comparison to the other five schools. One might phrase such a question in Passover-like form:[6] "How is Bowdoin different from all other schools?" A comparison between Bowdoin and the other schools, and

---

[6] One of the Passover questions is "Why is this night different from all other nights?"

hence the answer to this question, is shown in figure 1.4. This figure provides a dramatic summary of both the validity of the SAT (as scores go up, so too do first-year grades) and the remarkable homogeneity of its effect at all schools studied (the constancy of slope of all of the lines). The length of the line corresponds to the difference in SAT scores between those students who submitted them and those who did not; since Bowdoin has the greatest difference, it has the longest line. The slope of the line corresponds to the relationship between performance on the SAT and performance in first-year courses. These slopes are all about equal. The message is clear: If the goal of admissions policy is to admit students who are likely to do better in their college courses, students with higher SAT scores should be chosen over students with lower scores. Following such a rule is impossible if you do not require they submit their scores. Making the SAT optional seems to guarantee that it will be the lower-scoring students who withhold scores. And these lower-scoring students will also perform more poorly, on average, in their first-year college courses, even though the admissions office has found other evidence on which to offer them a spot.

This neatly brings us back to the moral of Thurber's fable recounted at the beginning of this chapter. The data allowing us to examine the

There is a well-known irony about selection: When a predictor variable is not used for selection, its predictive validity in the selected population increases. Thus we should expect the correlation between first-year grades and SAT scores to be higher among students who did not submit them than among those who did. To examine this pattern, I expanded the pool of schools studied, adding eighteen more to the ones so far examined. For these twenty-four schools I plotted the mean SAT score against mean first-year GPA for both those who submitted SAT scores and those who did not. The result is shown in figure 1.5. There is a significant increase in the correlation between SAT and first-year GPA (.89 vs. .80) among the students whose SAT scores were not used in their admission decision. This strongly suggests that schools that do not insist on the SAT are making decisions with larger errors than would otherwise be the case.

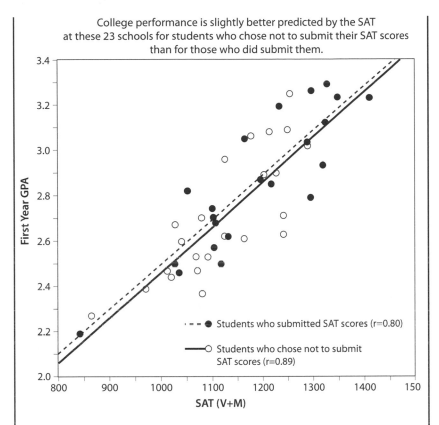

Figure 1.5. The first-year college grades for students who do not submit their SAT scores are predicted with greater accuracy from their SAT scores than they are for those students who submitted their SAT scores for admission.

efficacy of Bowdoin's admission policy are very difficult to obtain. Ordinarily, only the SAT scores of those students who have submitted them are readily available. It is rare to have access to the scores of the other students. Hence special attention should be paid when we do have them. The message of this study is inescapable—students who do not submit SAT scores withhold them because they do not reflect well on the students' ability to perform well in college. The SAT's predictions are borne out by these students' subsequent performance. Thus, schools that are contemplating adopting Bowdoin's policy would be well advised to hesitate. There is safety in caution.

2

⤳ ⤲

On Substituting Achievement Tests
for Aptitude Tests in College Admissions

Confucius has taught us that the first step toward wisdom is calling things by the right name. College admissions tests have historically been aptitude tests whose forebears were IQ tests. There are two principal reasons for this lineage:

1. The tests were designed to be fair to applicants from high schools of widely varying curricula.
2. Such tests have been remarkably successful in predicting success in undergraduate studies.

Thus it isn't surprising that the name of one such test reflects its history and its content—the Scholastic Aptitude Test.

Confucius would likely agree that a big step toward dishonesty is purposely naming something incorrectly. During the latter portion of the twentieth century the very notion of aptitude testing came under the fire of political correctness. Thus during the 1990s, when the Educational Testing Service (the organization that constructs, administers, and scores the SAT) struggled under the disastrous presidency of Nancy Cole, the name of the exam was changed to the redundant and virtually meaningless Scholastic Assessment Test. Happily, what the test tested remained staunchly the same. Most realized that Scholastic *Assessment* Test was an uninformative name, yet what could be inserted for the letter *A* that did not imply some characteristic of the examinee that was innate? The answer that is currently agreed upon (*developed*

The accuracy with which SAT scores predict freshman college grades is approximately the same as that of the high school grade point average. Considering that the former is a test taking less than three hours while the latter is a composite of exams, papers, projects, labs, and teacher observations produced over four years, the term *remarkable* is hardly hyperbole. In addition, while SAT scores may reflect various kinds of flaws in the test, these flaws can be detected and, over time, corrected. But high school grades are under no such control. Almost everyone agrees that there are teachers who through ignorance, stupidity, or venality give out biased grades. Yet there is no systematic way to discover and correct such biases. Thus, some observers might remark that it is amazing that high school grades predict college performance as well as they do. Perhaps it is the SAT that keeps high school grades honest—much as the scores on the National Assessment of Educational Progress (NAEP) have allowed us to uncover the biases in some state testing programs.

ability) suggests a combination of nature and nurture in unspecified proportions, but the resulting acronym *SDAT* would have been unpronounceable. And so the name of the test was changed again, this time reduced to the undefined *SAT*, no longer an acronym.

Now the National Association for College Admission Counseling has stepped in to help. The NACAC proposes that the admissions tests should be changed so that the *A* represents *Achievement*. But how, we may ask, can we do this, when there is a range of curricula across America's secondary schools? One solution is to restrict the content of the test to those aspects of the curricula that are universally shared. But this is hardly satisfactory if the goal of the test is to allow the students to demonstrate, as much as possible, the full range of what they know and can do. How much curriculum is common between a vocational high school and magnet school dedicated to science or the arts? Should the test focus on the lowest common denominator? Obviously this is not a happy solution. An alternative is to have a very large test (perhaps

lasting several days) that includes sections on an equally large array
of subjects. But which subjects? Chemistry and physics? What about
biology and earth science? Are we testing the students or the choices
that the schools make in the courses of study available? And so the
NACAC's suggested solution has devolved to be a set of achievement
tests from which students would pick a small subset, perhaps three or
four, that would allow them to demonstrate their mastery.

Is this a viable solution? At first blush it sounds reasonable. Students
who have focused their attention on the sciences might take a math and
a physics exam, those students more interested in the humanities might
take one in history and another in French, and all might be required to
take an exam in English. Then admissions committees would be able to
see each student at his or her best.

Could this work? The short answer is no. We will get to the details
next, but for those in too much of a hurry, consider the admission offi-
cer's task, which is trying to tell whether you are better in physics than
I am in French. Is such a comparison possible? Or reasonable? Was Babe
Ruth a better hitter than Mozart was a composer? At the extremes such
a judgment may be possible, for Babe Ruth was surely a better hitter
than Herbert Hoover was a president.[1] But admissions committees
must make choices between applicants who are much closer in their
accomplishments.

Currently there are achievement tests among the college admissions
battery (in addition to, not instead of, the usual aptitude tests). And
schools often require that students choose three that suit their training best. The scores on these tests seem comparable (the SAT-II consists of such tests, and are all scored on the familiar 200–800 scale).
Admissions committees often sum them together and make comparisons among students based on this sum. Doesn't this mean that somehow the magic of modern psychometrics can solve what seems like a
logically intractable problem? Alas, it cannot, as the rest of his chapter
demonstrates.[2]

---

[1] This was first established in 1930 by the Babe himself, who when asked about the
propriety of earning more money than the president of the United States replied, "I had
a better year than he did."

[2] I wish it were true, for it would provide a mechanism for resolving a recurring discussion my wife and I have had about whether Muhammad Ali was a better boxer than
George Kennan was a diplomat.

EQUATING: HOW TO COMPARE SCORES
THAT ARE NOT COMPARABLE

"Professor Wainer, will the test scores be curved?" I know of no teacher who has not heard something akin to this plaintive wail. What does it mean? Usually the student means, "Is there some way my 61 can become a B?" But a deeper question involves the underlying evidentiary support for deciding on the relationship between a specific numerical score and a letter grade. Why is 80 percent the lower bound for a B some of the time, and at other times 60 percent? It stems from the (often mistaken) notion that since ability follows a normal distribution (the "curve" in "curving the scores"), so too should test grades. Thus, this reasoning goes, we should distribute grades as a normal distribution, perhaps like the one shown in figure 2.1.

The distribution shown in figure 2.1 has an average score of 75 percent, which is classed as the middle of the C range. Suppose it represents accumulated test results, and that we give another test and the average score is 65 percent. If we assume that the class's ability distribution hasn't changed, the only remaining explanation is that the exam was more difficult than the earlier ones. And so to be fair we shift the grade categories downward 10 percentage points; a score of 70 percent, which used to be a low C, is now a low B. The grades have been curved. The curving of the scores allows us to compare performance across test administrations.

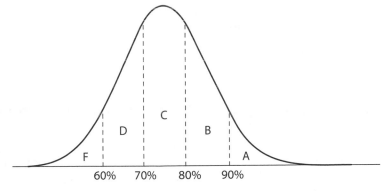

Figure 2.1. A normal distribution of course grades

Of course this logic is rarely swallowed whole, for if the average score on our new test is 85 percent, few teachers will curve scores downward. Thus they moot the whole point of curving. This is not an isolated instance of practical and political reality getting in the way of scientific probity.

The process of curving scores falls under the general heading of *test equating*, a subject taken very seriously indeed by major testing organizations. One of the causes of their concern is that for reasons of security, testing organizations use several (often very many) different forms of the same test, and they must equate them so that which form an examinee receives does not confer an advantage or impose a disadvantage over another examinee. In fact, the criterion for a successful equating of forms is that examinees, if they understood everything about the test construction and equating, would be indifferent about which form they received. To say it another way, successfully equated tests forms would yield the same score (on average) to someone regardless of which form he or she received.

When two different test forms are administered, however, the scores on one form are rarely the same as the scores on the other. Is this because one group of examinees is more able than the other? Or is one form more difficult than the other? Even if the average scores on the two forms are the same, it's possible that the lower ability of one group was just balanced out by the easier form it received.

How is equating accomplished? There are two broad categories of methodology—evidence based and faith based.

Evidence-based equating requires that the two test scores being equated share some common elements, either test items or test takers. If there are some common items, we can see if performance on those items was the same in both groups. If so, we infer that the two groups are of equal ability and so any difference we observe on the rest of the test must be due to differences in test difficulty. If performance is different on the common items (usually referred to as *anchor items* since they anchor the two forms to the same score scale), the size of the difference allows us to assess the difference in ability between the two groups and thus the difficulty of the rest of the test. Similarly if there is a subset of individuals who take both forms, we can scale the test scores so that their scores are the same, and the scaling function (the equating function) thus derived can be used to place all examinees on comparable scales.

Faith-based equating replaces data with assumptions. For example, we could assume that both examinee groups are of equal ability and so any differences observed are due to differential difficulty of the two forms. Or we can assume that both forms are of equal difficulty, and so any differences in scores observed are due to differences in group ability.

Faith-based methods are often used in international comparisons. For example, there is a Spanish language version of the SAT (Prueba de Aptitud Academica). A translation of the items in English is made with great care,[3] and it is assumed that the two forms are of equal difficulty, and so differences in performance are chalked up to lower ability of those taking the Spanish version. The alternative assumption is made in equating the French and English forms of the Canadian Forces Aptitude Test. Because it is assumed that the Francophone and Anglophone speakers are of equal ability, any differences in performance must be due to the differential difficulty of the test forms caused by differences in language.

There is convincing evidence that both assumptions are false, and that the truth almost surely lies somewhere in the middle. Such a middle road has been taken by Israel's National Institute for Testing and Evaluation (NITE) in its Psychometric Entrance Test. This exam is used to place examinees into various Israeli universities, and is given in nine languages. The NITE has strong evidence that the very act of translation changes the difficulty of the exam, and equally strong evidence that some groups of examinees are more able than others. Thus the NITE must find an evidenced-based method for equating. It accomplishes this by introducing two common elements: (1) all examinees who take a non-Hebrew-language form must also take a Hebrew proficiency exam, and (2) the performance in university coursework of previous examinees is used as an equating link. These two connecting links among the various test forms are a long way from perfect, but are a big step up from a strictly faith-based approach. The Israeli methodology is a partial solution to a difficult problem.

A fuller discussion of this issue is given in chapter 5.

---

[3] Actually not only is the translation done carefully, but equating studies are done with bilinguals who take both forms. But despite evidence that all bilinguals are better in one language than another, it is assumed that they are equally able in both.

Now let us return to the problem of equating scores among different achievement tests. Earlier I said that it was not possible to do so accurately enough for the purposes of college admission. Gainsaying this claim is the fact that all of the SAT II achievement tests are currently reported on the iconic College Board 200 to 800 scale. The fact that this has been done for decades—begging admissions committees to use them interchangeably to compare candidates—must mean that they are equated, doesn't it? They are not—the best that can be said is that they have been put on the same numerical scale (are "co-scaled"), but they are a long way from being equated.

What could having the same score on, say, a physics test and an French test mean? That these two people are equally good at their respective subjects? What could this possibly mean? How does Proust's knowledge of French match up with Einstein's understanding of physics? Clearly this is not a meaningful comparison. Perhaps it means that my ranking among people who took the physics exam is the same as your ranking among those who took French. This sort of matching is possible, but only meaningful if both groups of individuals are, in some sense, of equal ability.[4] And to determine if they are, we are back to Proust and Einstein again.

So how does the College Board (actually ETS) assign scores? The answer is akin to the Israeli procedure, a flawed solution to a difficult problem. A common link is used to co-scale the forms. A convenient common link for co-scaling achievement tests is the SAT-I, the aptitude test. It is convenient because, historically, virtually everyone who took the achievement tests also took the aptitude tests (though not vice versa). Happily, the SAT-Verbal has a moderate correlation with performance on achievement tests in many (but not all) of the humanities, while the SAT-Quantitative test has a similar relationship with achievement tests in the sciences and mathematics.

By using the SAT-I scores as a link, the scores of some of the achievement tests can be made approximately comparable. But there are distinct limitations. Among these are the following:

---

[4] This doesn't work even for subjects that are roughly comparable, like two different languages. It is well established that the average student who takes the SAT-II test in French would starve to death in a French restaurant, whereas the average person taking the comparable test in Hebrew, if dropped onto the streets of Tel Aviv, would do fine.

1. There remains no way of making effective comparisons between subjects in the humanities and the sciences. There is a positive correlation between SAT-Verbal and SAT-Quantitative, but it isn't strong enough to allow comparisons accurate enough for difficult admissions decisions.

2. Some subjects show no relationship between the achievement test and the allied SAT-I score. The SAT-II Spanish, for example, shows only a small relationship with the SAT-I. This likely reflects a substantial number of students whose home language is Spanish. This background may have a deleterious effect on their English language scores but boosts their Spanish scores. Hence it isn't surprising that they opt to include the Spanish achievement test in their admissions dossier. The same result is almost surely true for other immigrant language groups, but their numbers are too small to influence the overall results for that particular language test.

3. The accuracy of the co-scaling is crucially dependent on the strength of the relationship between the aptitude tests and the achievement test. Unless this relationship is very powerful indeed, comparisons across tests on different subjects will not be accurate enough for fair usage. Ironically, if this relationship were strong enough to make effective comparisons, we would have no need for the achievement tests.

DISCUSSION

Where does this leave us with respect to the NACAC recommendation that aptitude tests be replaced by achievement tests? First, even the rudimentary co-scaling now possible because almost all examinees who take achievement tests also take the same aptitude tests, would be impossible. The only option left would be scaling each examinee's test score relative to the others who took it. This could result in some examinees trying to game the system by choosing subjects that have the weakest pool of examinees—perhaps taking earth science instead of physics, French instead of Latin—rather than basing their choices solely on their own strengths and interests, making comparisons across areas less accurate still.

Second, by including examinee choice into the evaluation mix we introduce a new source of variability that almost surely would be unwelcome. As we will see in chapter 6, allowing choice exacerbates group differences in ways that are probably not valid.

In addition to technical arguments about the impossibility of making usefully accurate comparisons among students who present very different credentials for admission, there is also a serious logical problem. Suppose we were to take seriously the oft-stated goal of modern education—to produce graduates who, by virtue of being lifelong learners, will be able to continue to function at a high level in a fast-changing world. We thus want to admit students with the ability to learn what the school has to teach them, to foster skills that abet continued learning.

If we use achievement tests, from a high score we can infer that the student was able to learn that material. But a low score can reflect either the student's inability to learn or the school's inability to instruct. Or both. But should we assess this ability indirectly through achievement tests? Or directly through aptitude tests?

Thinking of the goal of education in an evidentiary way, if we wish to claim that "these students can learn what we want to teach them," what is stronger evidence to support this claim? A task that measures learning and reasoning ability directly? Or a test that measures knowledge of the Civil War?

Thus the obvious conclusion is that using only achievement tests for admissions decisions is either impossible or unnecessary. Suggesting that college admissions offices adopt this approach is irresponsible.

3

ᘓ ᘔ

On Rigid Decision Rules for Scholarships

The Preliminary SAT / National Merit Scholarship Qualifying Test (PSAT/NMSQT) is a program cosponsored by the College Board and the National Merit Scholarship Corporation. It's a standardized test that gives firsthand practice for the SAT. It also provides an opportunity to enter National Merit scholarship programs and gain access to college and career planning tools. It is taken by more than 1.5 million students annually.

The PSAT/NMSQT is designed to measure critical reading skills, math problem-solving skills, and writing skills. It is made up of relatively easy, retired SAT items and is dirt cheap to construct and administer. It also figures prominently in the third conclusion of the National Association for College Admission Counseling's report in September 2008 on admissions testing. The NACAC recommends that the use of the PSAT with a rigid qualification cut-score for such programs as the National Merit scholarships be immediately halted.

The NACAC supports this recommendation (demand?) by pointing out that requiring a cut-score to qualify for a scholarship (and by generalization, for anything) leaves no room for human judgment at the boundary. All sensible people would agree that there is insufficient information to conclude that someone just above the decision boundary is more worthy than someone else just below it.

Yet with limited resources, triage decisions must be made.

The problem with a hard-and-fast cut-score is one that has plagued testing for more than a century. The Indian civil service system, on which the American civil service system was based, found a clever way around it. The passing mark to qualify for consideration for a civil service position was 20. But if you received a 19 you were given one "honor point" and qualified. If you scored 18 you were given two honor points, and again qualified. If you scored 17, you were given three honor points, and you still qualified for further consideration. But if you scored 16 you did not qualify, for you were four points away. I don't know exactly what the logic was behind this system, but I might guess that experience had shown that anyone scoring below 17 was sufficiently unlikely to be successful in obtaining a position, that it was foolish to include them in the competition. But having a sharp break at 16 might have been thought too abrupt, and so the method of honor points was concocted.

How does this compare with the Merit Scholarship program? The initial screening selects 15,000 (the top 1 percent) from the original pool of one and a half million who take the PSAT. These 15,000 are then screened much more carefully using both the SAT and ancillary information to select the 1,500 winners of a scholarship (the top 10 percent of the 15,000 semifinalists). Once this process is viewed as a whole, several things become obvious:

1. Since the winners are in the top 0.1 percent of the population, it is dead certain they are all enormously talented individuals.
2. Many worthy individuals are missed, but that is inevitable if there is only money for 1,500 winners.
3. Expanding the initial semifinal pool by even a few points will expand the pool of semifinalists enormously (the normal curve grows exponentially at that point), and those given the equivalent of some PSAT "honor points" are extraordinarily unlikely to win anyway, given the strength of the competition. It would also increase the cost of the final screening apace.

What about making the screening more rigorous—rather than using the PSAT scores alone? Such a screening must be more expensive, and to employ it as widely would, I suspect, use up much more of the available resources, leaving less money for the actual scholarships. The irony is that utilizing a system like that proposed by the NACAC would either have to be much more limited in its initial reach, or it would have to content itself with giving out many fewer scholarships.

Of course, one could argue that more money should be raised to do a better job in initial screening. I would argue that if more money were available, the current method of allocating it should be continued and used to either give out more scholarships, or bigger ones.

This completes the explication behind my initial conclusion that some of the recommendations of the NACAC make sense only if you say them fast. Relying on evidence in the evaluation of policy proposals makes decisions wiser, if for no other reason than it forces you to slow down a bit.

In the past three chapters I have presented evidence that a general aptitude test has many advantages over suggested alternatives. As an illustrative example I have used the SAT and its junior partner, the PSAT. In chapter 4 I will go further and show in some detail how the use of such tests can provide important help in the triage decisions that are inevitable in public education, when limited resources must be allocated to overwhelming need.

4

༄ ༄

The Aptitude-Achievement Connection

Using an Aptitude Test to Aid
in Allocating Educational Resources

In chapter 3 we learned that the PSAT, the shorter and easier version of the SAT, can be used effectively as one important part of selection decisions for scholarships. In this chapter we expand on this discussion to illustrate that the PSAT also provides evidence that can help us allocate scarce educational resources. We will look in a different, but allied arena: admission decisions for high school advanced placement courses.

One of the lasting success stories in American education is the College Board's Advanced Placement (AP) program. It originally allowed only a small elite to take advanced courses in high school and thus to obtain college credit. However, the program has taken on a life of its own and spread widely in American high schools. The number of participants has doubled every ten years. Today more than half of American high schools and a third of four-year college-bound seniors participate in this burgeoning program. Whereas overall assessments of American public schools range from highly critical[1] to favorable, even optimistic,[2] all sides give AP their approval. A major strength of AP and a possible reason for its success is its eschewing fads for a solid

---

This chapter developed from W. Lichten and H. Wainer, "The Aptitude-Achievement Function: An Aid for Allocating Educational Resources, with an Advanced Placement Example," *Educational Psychology Review* 12(2) (2000): 201–228.

[1] National Committee on Excellence in Education 1983; Ravitch 1985; Finn 1991.

[2] Carson, Huelskamp, and Woodall 1993; Bracey 1991; 1998.

collaboration between high school teachers and college professors, with an emphasis on subject content.

A growing number of states support it in many ways, including paying student fees, requiring all high schools to offer AP courses, appropriating funds for AP, supporting teacher training for AP, compelling state colleges and universities to accept for credit AP grades of 3 or higher, and requiring AP students to take the national examination. Five civil rights organizations have sued the University of California on behalf of black, Hispanic, and Filipino-American students charging discriminatory admissions policies, based on the practice of giving credit to college applicants for AP courses, which are less available to minority students.[3]

The very popularity of the Advanced Placement program means we are faced with a problem. The rigor of the material within AP courses means that they may not be suitable for all students. Moreover, because of the special training required for AP teachers and the smallish class sizes, there is often limited availability. How is a school district to decide how many AP classes make sense for its student body? And who among their students would benefit most from such courses? The answers to these important and difficult questions ought to be based on evidence, and the evidence that can help us answer both questions is aptitude test scores. We should base our choice of specific aptitude test on both validity and convenience. An invalid test does no one good, nor does any measure that is too expensive of time or of treasure. I will show that the SAT and its derivative, the PSAT, are fine choices.

In the more than eighty years since the Scholastic Aptitude Test was first added to the College Board's Admission Testing Program its character has remained remarkably constant. In fact, Carl Brigham's decision in 1929 to meld its six subtests into two separate scores, measuring respectively verbal and mathematical aptitude, yielded a test that bears a striking similarity to that which is familiar to many of today's high school seniors. Although the original SAT, a direct lineal descendent of a mass-administered standardized test of "general intelligence," is very similar to its current namesake, the interpretation of its scores has changed. No longer are SAT scores viewed as an immutable result of innate ability, but rather as a complex mixture of inputs from both nature and nurture.

---

[3] Nieves 1999; Rosenfeld 1999; *Jesus Rios et al vs. Regents of the University of California*, Case C. 99-0525, U.S. District Court, Northern District of California.

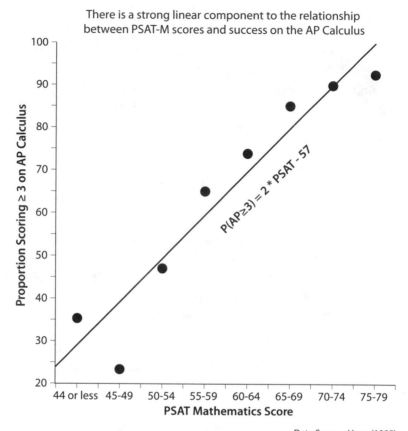

Figure 4.1. A rough estimate of the relationship between performance on the PSAT-Math test and the likelihood of a score of 3 or greater on the AP Calculus test. Based on a sample of about 1,000 students (Haag 1985). As we will see in figure 4.3, this relationship is described better with the non-linear connecting function that is only hinted at here.

Figure 4.1 is a plot, based on a relatively small data set, that shows a strong linear component in the relationship between performance on the PSAT-Mathematics test and the probability of obtaining a minimally passing score of 3 or greater[4] on the AP Calculus AB exam over most

[4] A score of 3 on an AP exam is a criterion used by many colleges and universities to indicate performance that is good enough to justify being granted credit for that subject as a college course. In this chapter I use the Calculus AB (first semester) and Calculus BC (first and second semester) tests for a case study. Typically, of the approximately 2.6

of the range of the data. Once that relationship is nailed down with a more extensive data-gathering effort, it would be straightforward to exploit the empirical relationship between performance on aptitude and achievement tests to provide educational resources in a more efficacious manner. It can also help us to understand some schools' unexpected achievements.

The 1988 movie *Stand and Deliver* chronicled the remarkable success the students of Jaime Escalante, a math teacher in Garfield High School in Los Angeles, had on the AP Calculus test. In the next section I explicate Escalante's efforts, using the school's results on an aptitude test to provide context. Next I contrast two quite different school districts:

1. La Cañada, an upscale Los Angeles suburb with a single high school in which sixty-four out of the sixty-six students who took the AP Calculus examination passed it.
2. The city of Detroit, with a much larger school population that is overwhelmingly African-American and low income, and with twenty-three high schools in which a total of eighty-nine students took the AP Calculus exam, of whom fifty-eight passed.[5]

All of these apparently discrepant results are predictable from advance information. I will illustrate how this information can guide school officials to make good use of limited resources.

CALCULUS, GARFIELD HIGH SCHOOL, AND MIRACLES

Miracles abound in the Holy Bible. David Hume (1955) forcefully debunked such events as "a violation of the laws of nature ... [p]resented to us by a barbarous and ignorant people." Hume's contemporary, Immanuel Kant (1793), more tactfully answered the question of miracles by pointing out that they seemed to occur relatively often in

---

million seniors graduating from high school in the United States, annually about 90,000 (3 percent) will pass one of these AP calculus examinations at a level of 3 or higher.

[5] Detroit is as segregated as any major city in the United States (Massey and Denton 1993). It has almost no immigrant school population. Its selective schools, the only ones with successful AP students, have the same racial composition as the city as a whole.

ancient times, but had become much rarer recently. Indeed, ever since these philosophers showed the contradiction between miracles and the skeptical empiricism of science, the former have occurred less often—with one exception. Miracles appear to happen almost every day in American education. Let me relate the story of one such wonder, then examine it within the context of additional empirical evidence.

In 1988 the film *Stand and deliver* told the inspiring story of Jaime Escalante, a math teacher at Garfield High School. As depicted in the film, Garfield was an educationally marginal, inner-city school with a largely Latino student population. The film suggested that Garfield was a home for the kinds of low achievement and high dropout rates that satisfy the common stereotype. Into this miasma stepped Jaime Escalante, a hardworking and idealistic math teacher who through the force of his own will dragged a collection of Garfield students down a mathematical path that ended with their successfully completing a course in college-level calculus and passing the AP Calculus exam. This initial success inspired future generations of Garfield students to take AP Calculus, at one point making Garfield one of the leading performers on this test in the entire country. The truth, though less dramatic, is more instructive and equally inspiring.

In 1986, 129 Garfield students took the AP Calculus AB examination and 85 (66 percent) passed it, to put Garfield fourth in the country,[6] a remarkable accomplishment. How did Escalante do it? There are two obvious answers. First he recruited the 129 students who took the exam, and second he taught them enough calculus to allow them to pass it. This partitioning of the task into two parts, recruitment and teaching, provides a guide to the analysis. Let us begin with recruitment.

In 1986, 270 Garfield seniors, 34 percent of the class, took the SAT and had an average math score of 410. To proceed with the analysis I make the simple assumptions that Garfield High School is the same as the rest of the country in three respects:

1. The relationship between PSAT and SAT scores
2. The conditional distribution of SAT scores around the mean
3. The relationship between PSAT and AP tests

[6] Mathews 1988.

TABLE 4.1
The Predicted Performance of Students
from Garfield High School on AP Calculus

PSAT Score	Predicted percentage scoring 3 or more on AP Calculus	Expected number in Garfield High School	Expected number in Escalante's class	Expected number passing AP Calculus
75–79	93	0	0	0
70–74	89	1	1	1
65–69	85	2	2	2
60–64	74	7	7	5
55–59	65	17	17	11
50–54	48	31	31	15
45–49	23	46	46	11
44 or less	35	166	25	9
TOTAL		270	129	53

Last, I assume that the 129 students that Escalante recruited were the best from the senior class.

These assumptions yield the results in table 4.1, which summarizes the analysis. The first two columns merely represent what was shown graphically in figure 4.1.[7] The third column is derived from the cumulative normal distribution with mean of 410 and standard deviation of 100 (assumption 2). Column 4 simply chooses the top scoring students at Garfield for Escalante's class; and the last column multiplies column 4 by column 2 (assumptions 1 and 3) and rounds. Thus the overall prediction is that approximately fifty-three students from Escalante's class would be expected to score 3 or more on AP Calculus.

But eighty-five passed. This is thirty-two more than what is expected from this normative analysis. This prediction is based on national averages. Courses that are better than average will do better. Courses that are worse than average will do worse. We can characterize the "excess" passing of thirty-two students as the *Escalante effect*.

[7] Figure 4.1 is derived from a smallish sample of barely more than 1,000 AP examinees and exhibits some curious anomalies; nevertheless they are sufficient for the Garfield High School data. The remaining examples use the much more extensive data ($n = 94,000$) reported in 1997 by Wayne Camara of The College Board.

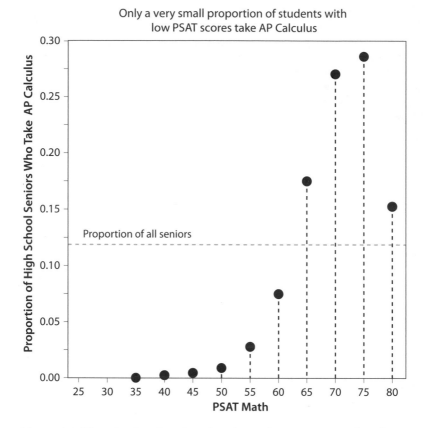

Figure 4.2. The selection function that shows the proportion of students who took the AP Calculus examination in 1997 as a function of their PSAT-Mathematics score

The Escalante effect encompasses both impressive teaching and recruiting. As is evident in table 4.1, I assumed that he recruited from the top down in Garfield High School and got everyone. This is in sharp contrast with what is observed nationally. Figure 4.2 shows the proportion of students who take the AP Calculus exam nationally as a function of PSAT score. Aside from the anomalous downturn at the high end, we see a steady increase in the likelihood of taking this exam with performance on the PSAT. But only a small proportion of students with PSAT scores below 60 take the test; the proportion of students whose PSAT scores are below 50 who take it is minuscule. Escalante not only

recruited students below this threshold, but also managed to get a substantial proportion of them to pass the exam. The results displayed in
this figure will be important in understanding subsequent outcomes.

This analysis helps us to understand the size of the miracle at Garfield High School. Jaime Escalante did not turn straw into gold—he had
a cadre of some good students. But he did somehow elicit from them
very impressive efforts. We must also credit Escalante with extraordi-
nary efforts at recruitment. Of course, our assumption of his having
recruited the best students at Garfield High School may be somewhat
wrong, in which case Escalante gets more credit as a teacher and less as
a recruiter. But these results derive from the most likely scenario.

For further insight, let us consider Garfield High School in 1997, six
years after Escalante resigned his position there. Instead of eighty-five,
the number of passing grades in AP Calculus had shrunk to nineteen,
less than 3 percent of the graduating class. Part of this shrinkage is
due to the loss of a gifted recruiter and teacher, but a substantial part
was due to the shifting character of the student body of Garfield High
School. This aspect was predicted by Garfield's declining scores on
mathematics aptitude tests.

In 1987 the school's standardized mathematics achievement scores
were at the 53rd percentile. These dropped steadily to the 37th percentile in 1993 and at the 24th percentile in spring of 1998.[8] Over the same
period the SAT-Mathematics scores suffered a consistent and parallel
decline of more than 50 points. Based upon this new distribution of
student ability, we would predict that twenty-four students at Garfield could pass AP Calculus, close to the actual number (nineteen)
that passed.

To place Escalante's accomplishment in a broader perspective, and to
demonstrate another use for this prediction technology, let us consider
the size of the potential audience for an AP Calculus class at a high-performing suburban high school. Not far from Garfield High School, in an
upscale suburb of Los Angeles, is La Cañada High School. La Cañada is
near the top of a common "citation index" for effective advanced placement teaching, with 2 AP tests taken per graduating senior. La Cañada
had 232 SAT test takers in 1998, with an average math score of 605.

---

[8] Estimates based on California Learning Assessment System scores.

TABLE 4.2
The Predicted Performance of Students from
La Cañada High School on AP Calculus

PSAT Score	Predicted percentage scoring 3 or more on AP Calculus	Expected number in La Cañada High School	Expected number passing AP Calculus
80–76	97.1	20	19
75–71	92.1	22	20
70–66	82.1	33	27
65–61	68.3	41	28
60–56	52.9	41	22
55–51	38.2	33	13
50–46	24.5	22	5
45–41	15.6	12	2
40–36	9.1	5	0
35–31	6.0	2	0
30–26	9.2	1	0
25–20	0.0	0	0
TOTAL		232	137

Making the same assumptions as we did with Garfield High School, we obtain the potential results shown in table 4.2.

Table 4.2 is identical in formation to table 4.1 except that the relationship between AP scores and PSAT scores has been updated. This update reflects much greater stochastic stability, since it is based on a sample of 94,000 students that the College Board's Wayne Camara[9] published. Its precision is an order of magnitude greater than the function shown in figure 4.1. It also reflects the recentering of PSAT scores that took place in 1995. Shown in figure 4.3 is the updated analog to figure 4.1. The solid points are the empirical results; the small dots are from the interpolating function fitted to those points. As is easily seen, the model fits like a glove. I used this revised functional relation to obtain the results shown in table 4.2.

This suggests that La Cañada has the student potential for 137 students to take and pass the AP Calculus (assuming a course no more nor

[9] Camara 1997.

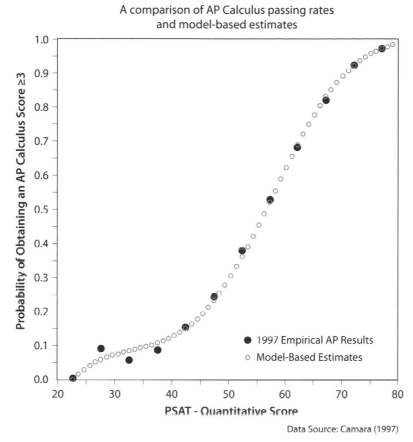

A comparison of AP Calculus passing rates
and model-based estimates

Data Source: Camara (1997)

Figure 4.3 An estimate of the relationship between performance on the
PSAT-Math test and the likelihood of a score of 3 or greater on the AP
Calculus test. Based on a sample of about 94,000 students.

less effective than the national average). In fact, sixty-four did pass this
exam, 47 percent of the potential number. The difference between what
could have happened and what did happen is surely the result of both
recruitment and teaching. Recruitment for AP Calculus at La Cañada
faces a different challenge than at Garfield—the number of AP courses
offered means a competition for the most able students. In addition,
and of at least equal importance, La Cañada sharply restricts enrollment in AP courses to students who are virtually certain to pass the

exam (the typical pass rate in AP Calculus is 97 percent). The disparity between the number who pass the exam and the potential number who could have passed it suggests the enrollment in AP Calculus is overly restrictive; that with both appropriate resources and encouragement, La Cañada's AP Calculus program could be substantially enlarged. Yet the strategy of limiting enrollment to students who are very likely to pass is one way to allocate resources effectively. As we shall see in the next example, the city of Detroit follows much the same strategy, but in a different way.

CALCULUS AND THE POTENTIAL OF DETROIT

The principal point of this chapter is that the evidence provided by the empirical relationship between aptitude and achievement test scores provides a context for understanding the test results. This increase in understanding can allow a more efficacious allocation of students to classes. The AP Calculus results for the city of Detroit are our third illustration of how this technique can be used. This example reflects an important variation from the two examples discussed in the previous section; few students in Detroit take either the SAT or the PSAT.

Detroit is a city with highly segregated schools that are 95 percent African-American. In 1997 approximately 5,000 students graduated from city schools. Of these students, only fifty-eight passed the AP calculus examination. Fifty-eight passing AP scores out of a student pool of 5,000 seems like a small number. But Detroit is not La Cañada in either the average performance of its student body or in the resources available for their education. We need to know what is the size of the available pool of students suitable for AP classes, for it is against this base that we should evaluate the efficacy of Detroit's AP programs. Because few students in Detroit take the SAT, other information is needed to estimate the size of the pool of qualified AP test takers.

I used the mathematics portion of both the Michigan State High School Proficiency test and the Metropolitan 7 test scores to find where Detroit's students' stand. They are well below the national average, and

TABLE 4.3
The Predicted Performance of High School Students
from Detroit on AP Calculus   ·

PSAT score	Predicted percentage scoring 3 or more on AP Calculus	Predicted PSAT distribution in Detroit high schools	Expected number (assuming 100% recruitment)	Passing AP Calculus[a]
80–76	97.1	1	1	0
75–71	92.1	5	5	1
70–66	82.1	15	12	4
65–61	68.3	41	28	6
60–56	52.9	92	49	4
55–51	38.2	165	63	2
50–46	24.5	243	60	2
45–41	15.6	292	46	1
40–36	9.1	289	26	0
35–31	6.0	229	14	0
30–26	9.2	149	14	0
25–20	0.0	130	0	0
TOTAL		**1,651**	**316**	**20**

[a] Recruitment as per national averages (figure 4.2).

a little lower than the position of African-American students nation-wide on the SAT and PSAT. From the average of both state test scores we would estimate a mean math PSAT score of 42.[10] Combining this result with the national estimate that 30 percent of African-American students take the PSAT yields the estimated PSAT distribution shown in the third column of table 4.3.

We can predict that, based upon the imputed PSAT score distribution of the approximately 1,650 Detroit students anticipated to take the PSAT, 316 (about 20 percent) would pass the AP Calculus test. That

[10] I recognize that this bit of inference must be considered rough because of the self-selected nature of the SAT populations as contrasted with the almost total enumeration of the citywide testing. My estimate rests squarely on the assumption that for the most part the same selection process that operates nationally would operate in Detroit in determining which 30 percent of the students in Detroit will take the PSAT. This assumption is untestable, but seems plausible enough for this application. It is important, however, not to take these estimates too literally.

fifty-eight did pass the test suggests that there is a potential demand for an expanded AP Calculus program within Detroit.[11]

But what is likely to be the cost of servicing this demand? Table 4.4 enumerates the Detroit students who took the AP Calculus test in 1997, broken down by their high school and the grade they achieved on the AP Calculus test. We see that there is a reasonably high success rate among Detroit's students who take AP Calculus, but this is surely due to the very selective nature of the schools that offer the course.[12] I include the 1997 performance of La Cañada and Garfield High Schools, as well as the nation as a whole, for comparison.[13] Does it make sense, in view of the number of Detroit students who might profitably take AP Calculus, for the schools to expand this course offering?

For this question table 4.3 becomes an important tool indeed. School programs are always the result of a series of triage decisions. Limited resources mean that choices must be made. Consider the entries in table 4.3 and note that as the PSAT-M score decreases, the "yield" of passing scores decreases as well. Students whose PSAT-M scores are below 55 have considerably less than a fifty-fifty chance of passing the exam. Is it sensible to provide a course that is so poorly aimed at the students in it? Would it be a better use of resources to provide a more suitable course for the students who do not show the necessary aptitude?

[11] Of course this sort of result is a chimera when one considers the selection function (figure 4.2). Based on this function, virtually no one with PSAT score lower than 50 would take the course, and so the hypothetical situation expressed here is wildly optimistic. A more plausible estimate of the number who would pass, based on current enrollment likelihoods, is closer to 30 than 300. Thus the accomplishment of Detroit's schools in producing 58 students who passed the AP Calculus test suggests either much better recruiting into AP classes than is represented by the national average, or much better instruction, or both.

[12] There are twenty-three high schools in Detroit, which makes for an average of about fourteen students per school who could potentially pass the AP Calculus exam. This is hardly the critical mass for an effective AP program. Consequently, Detroit, like many city systems, relies on specialized college preparatory high schools, which admit students on application and by entrance examinations. Historically these are Cass Technical and Renaissance High Schools, with a recent upgrading of Martin Luther King High School to magnet school status. As seen in table 4.4, all three have successful AP math programs.

[13] These figures are for both AP courses, Calculus AB (equivalent to a one semester college course) and Calculus BC (equivalent to a full year's course). All the students in Detroit took AB, as did most of the students at Garfield and two-thirds of the students at La Cañada. Nationally 80 percent of those taking AP Calculus elect AB.

TABLE 4.4

The Performance of High School Students from the City of Detroit, as well as La Cañada and Garfield High Schools on AP Calculus.

AP Calculus test score	Detroit High Schools			Detroit total	La Cañada	Garfield	National[a]
	Cass	ML King	Renaissance				
5	1	1	3	5	32	3	28,756
4	4	3	11	18	16	4	32,587
3	20	6	9	35	16	12	37,811
2	13	4	2	19	2	14	23,558
1	10	2	0	12	0	28	22,047
TOTAL	48	16	25	89	66	61	144,759
Number ≥3	25	10	23	58	64	19	99,154
Percent ≥ 3	52%	63%	92%	65%	97%	31%	68%

[a] National results included for purposes of comparison.

This is clearly the approach taken by both Detroit, where AP Calculus is only given at a few, highly selective high schools, and at La Cañada, in which students are not permitted to take AP Calculus unless they are almost certain to pass.

The approach taken here can even provide some information on the quality of instruction. For example, it appears that the three elite Detroit high schools admit students to AP Calculus who score above the 80th percentile based on national norms. This means that this distribution of ability in those schools can be well represented as a normal distribution, which (on the PSAT scale) is cut off below a score of 59. If we assume that the eighty-nine students who elected to take AP Calculus were the top eighty-nine students attending these schools, we would expect, from national results, that fifty-eight would score 3 or better, exactly what occurred. From this we infer that the instruction that they received was at a par with the average AP Calculus course given elsewhere in the country. The La Cañada 97 percent pass rate implies that the instruction is considerably better than average. Note, however, that, based on the passing rate, the instruction in Detroit's Renaissance High School is roughly of the same quality.

EXTENSIONS, GENERALIZATIONS, AND A CAVEAT

The race is not always to the swift, nor the battle to
the strong; but that's the way to lay your bets.
—Ring Lardner

The previous section ended with the educational equivalent of realpolitik. But it was not my intention to be harsh, only practical. Consider the augmented version of table 4.3 shown as table 4.5. The first four columns of this table show how many are at the score shown in the first column *or above*. The fifth column (number of classes needed) simply divides the number in column 3 by twenty (a plausible approximate size for an AP Calculus class). Thus, if the course is limited to only those whose PSAT-M score is 66 or above, only twenty-one would qualify and hence one class would suffice, whereas if open enrollment is chosen and all 1,651 students who anticipate going to college enroll, it would require eighty-three classes.[14] The sixth column (number of successes per class) divides the predicted number passing at each level by the number of classes. Thus, once again, if a PSAT-M score of 66 or above is required for registration in the course, we would expect eighteen students (86 percent) in that one class to pass. But if all took it, the pass rate (the "yield") drops to only four per class (19 percent). Last, if we assume that the annual per pupil expenditure is $6,000 and that each student takes six classes, the cost per class per student is $1,000. Using this ball-park figure allows us to estimate how much it costs for each passing score, depending on where the cut-score for taking AP Calculus is set. We see that with a cut-score at 66 the cost of each passing score is only $1,167, whereas with open enrollment it could be as high as $5,192. For purposes of generalization keep in mind that the ratio between these two figures remains the same regardless of the actual costs.

Limiting enrollment to a course based upon a student's likely success in it is hardly a radical idea, yet turning down an interested student is never a happy decision. The impact of an enrollment limitation on an affected student can be ameliorated if an attractive alternative can be provided. Once again, a reanalysis of Camara's results provides us with just such an option. Not all AP exams are equally difficult. Some are markedly easier to pass. As an example, consider the comparison between the ability-achievement functions for AP Calculus and AP Psychology shown in figure 4.4. The best predictor for AP Psychology is PSAT-Verbal and a score of 41 on that test portends a 50 percent probability of passing the AP Psychology exam. This is almost two standard deviations lower than the score (on PSAT-Math) required for the same likelihood of success in AP Calculus.[15] At present, psychology might not be a realistic choice for a school, because few faculty are prepared to teach such a course. In the long run, because psychology is so popular a major in college, one could foresee this subject entering the high school curriculum and faculty repertoire. At any rate, among the more

---

[14] Once again, this is hardly a likely outcome (in the entire United States only 1,680 students with PSAT scores below 40 took AP Calculus). My goal here is merely to show what would happen if everyone took AP Calculus.

[15] This calculation assumes that the scales of the two portions of the PSAT are roughly comparable. This assumption is credible because the same people take both parts, and the same number of points on each scale relate to approximately the same number of people.

TABLE 4.5
The Detroit Predictions from Table 4.3 Shown as Cumulants
and Augmented with Some Plausible Costs

PSAT-M score	Percentage scoring ≥3 on AP Calculus	Predicted PSAT distribution in Detroit high schools	Number passing AP Calculus	Number of classes needed	Number of successes per class	Cost per passing score
≥66	86%	21	18	1	17	$1,167
≥61	74%	62	46	3	15	$1,348
≥56	62%	154	95	8	12	$1,621
≥51	50%	319	158	16	10	$2,019
≥46	39%	562	218	28	8	$2,578
≥41	31%	854	264	43	6	$3,235
≥36	25%	1,143	290	57	5	$3,941
≥31	22%	1,372	304	69	4	$4,513
≥26	21%	1,521	318	76	4	$4,783
≥20	19%	1,651	318	83	4	$5,192

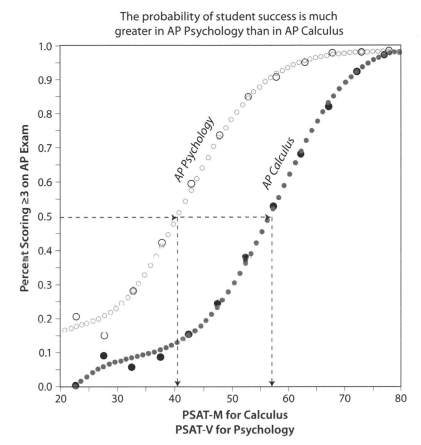

Figure 4.4. An estimate of the relationship between performance on PSAT tests and the likelihood of a score of 3 or greater on the AP Calculus and the AP Psychology test. Based on a sample of about 94,000 students.

than thirty different AP exams offered, there is likely to be something of suitable difficulty for a wide range of student and faculty abilities.[16]

It would be straightforward to prepare a set of tables, each parallel to table 4.5, that chronicle the expenses associated with each AP course.

[16] An interesting example of this sort of strategy is seen at Garfield High School since Escalante's retirement. Escalante opened the school's eyes to AP possibilities, and the school responded by broadening the number of AP courses offered. Consequently the decline in the number of students who passed AP Calculus is counterbalanced by the 109 (out of 112) who passed AP Spanish.

Using such tables, one could balance admission rules for courses with budget limitations and student demand. This would allow school administrators to maximize student success within the existing practical constraints of available resources (e.g., money, space, teachers) and talent.

This brief financial analysis shows the cost of various kinds of policies associated with admission to AP courses. Crucial to this analysis is the ability to stratify the student population by PSAT scores. Obviously this is not the only measure that could be used for this purpose; it is merely a cheap, handy, and efficacious one.

The PSAT (or any other well-constructed ability test that can be equated to it) is a practical choice. Furthermore, it is a better predictor of AP performance than high school grades or performance in courses with the same subject matter.[17] Nevertheless, other factors, such as student motivation, teacher evaluations, and grades certainly could play a role in determining who takes the AP courses. Finally, there may be intangible benefits for students who take the course and do not receive a grade of 3 or higher.[18]

Only hinted at here are many potential uses of the handy empirical relationship between student performance on aptitude and achievement tests. It is beyond my immediate goal to provide an encyclopedic presentation. Rather I wish to show how the evidence conveyed in this relationship can be exploited to help in understanding, and through rational management improving, educational performance.

National Projection

The film *Stand and Deliver* about Escalante's success became AP's "most effective promotional device. If barrio children could successfully conquer AP calculus, why couldn't everyone?"[19] Of course, as figure 4.3 shows, not everyone can conquer calculus; nevertheless, Escalante opened our eyes to possibilities that had previously been neglected. We ask the question, how far could America push the expansion of the AP program? National figures show that of the 114,318 students who

[17] Camara and Millsap 1998.
[18] For a related discussion, see Heubert and Hauser 1999.
[19] Mathews 1998.

took the Calculus AB or BC exams in 1997, 75,000 achieved a score of 3 or higher. However, there were 1,120,000 seniors who took the SAT, with an average math score of 511. From figure 4.4, we would predict that 407,000 could score 3 or higher on the AP Calculus exam. *American high school students have the capability of quintupling the current rate of passing the AP calculus examination.*[20] Thus Garfield Senior High School pointed the way, not only to higher achievement in a barrio school, but in the nation at large. That the actual number of passing scores in Garfield exceeded the predicted value is a testimony to Escalante's teaching.

Another Escalante Effect

In 1997, a few nonselective high schools in Detroit offered AP calculus courses in which no student achieved a passing grade, presumably because the selective schools have skimmed off the top layer of students, so that the remaining students were unable to succeed in the AP math program. This is a less positive "Escalante effect," which raised unrealistic expectations. It might be wiser for such schools to begin AP with a course that is more in line with the capabilities of their students and faculty. I have included a semigraphical display in the appendix to this chapter that connects PSAT level with AP course. Using such a guide might help school administrators to decide on course offerings.

A Caveat

Not all AP tests exhibit a strong relationship with the PSAT. Less related are foreign language exams; least related among these is AP Spanish. Shown in figure 4.5 is the plot of PSAT-Verbal scores against AP Spanish Literature performance. It seems clear that those students who take the AP Spanish Literature test perform rather well, and that

---

[20] Of course this again is a wildly optimistic and expensive estimate based on everyone taking AP Calculus. But it allows us to place a cost estimate on suggestions akin to those of University of Chicago scholar Benjamin Bloom about the possibilities that appear if the admission gates to courses of study are widened.

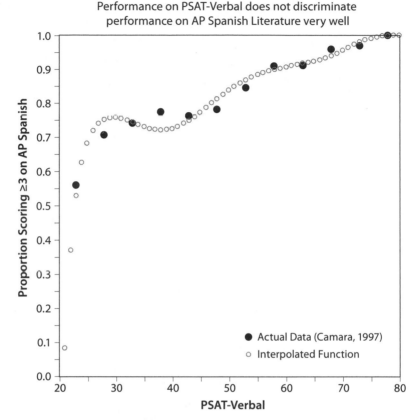

Figure 4.5. An estimate of the relationship between performance on PSAT-Verbal test and the likelihood of a score of 3 or greater on the AP Spanish Language test in 1997. It shows only a very modest relationship between performance on the two tests.

how well they perform has little to do with how well they perform on the PSAT-Verbal.[21]

Thus, happily, when this methodology does not work, it tells you. Had we used each student's Social Security number instead of the PSAT score to predict AP performance, we would have found a horizontal

[21] The famous psychologist George Miller once told me that the ability to learn a language has little to do with intelligence. To support this he pointed to Holland, where "everyone can speak English, even dumb people." He then expanded with an evolutionary argument pointing out that in prehistory those people who couldn't understand "Look out for the tiger" rarely lived to reproduce.

function. If one is interested in using the approach I am advocating to aid in the allocation of educational resources, we must look carefully at these connective functions. The PSAT is wonderfully useful most of the time—but not always.

Summing Up the Pieces Needed for Measuring School Performance

To predict or understand the performance of a school as a whole on AP courses involves more than data like those in these tables in this chapter. One needs other components described in the ensuing paragraphs.

1. *An explicit definition of the outcome of interest*. This is obvious, but since there are at least two somewhat separate definitions in current use, I explicitly defined the success of a school or system by the proportion of students who pass the AP examinations (score at a level of 3 or higher) and *not* by its AP participation rate.

2. *A characterization of student ability*. Success on any AP examination depends heavily on the ability of the students taking it. This, in turn, depends on many factors beyond the school's control. Thus to be able to accurately characterize how well a school is doing, we must take into account the preparation of that school's students. In this chapter I have characterized that preparation by the SAT/PSAT score distribution.

3. *A functional connection between success and qualifications*. The fitting of a mathematical model to Wayne Camara's results allowed us to calculate the probability of success for the students in question, based on their PSAT scores.

4. *A model for the selection of students into AP courses*. As we illustrated, a "top down" system of student selection is the most likely model for almost all schools. Thus a school gauges its resources: the numbers of qualified teachers, of classes it can support (AP classes usually require smaller class size and extra energy and time on the part of all involved), and of able and motivated students. Then, given these numbers, the school selects its most qualified students to try to fulfill two not completely compatible goals: a high success rate and offering the course to the maximum number of students who wish it. I used a sharp truncation point here but a fuzzier decision rule could be used, although if it is, this methodology will allow us to calculate

the cost of such a decision rule. Perhaps the Indian notion of "honor points" could be useful.

5. *A measure of teaching and motivation.* When all these factors are weighed as well as possible, there are still the intangibles of the quality of the teachers and of the students' motivation. These factors are not always apparent in the cold statistics available to us. But we can begin to gauge their effects through the use of this evidence-based methodology.

CONCLUSION

There are no miracles in education. As Hume pointed out, educational "miracles" are either the result of deception or can be understood through the framework of scientific inquiry. The high performance of Escalante's students reflected his exceptional drive and talent as a teacher, but they were not miraculous. The school climate for learning and its high level of aspiration, which has outlasted Escalante at Garfield High School, deserve credit as well.

The PSAT played a useful role in understanding and predicting performance on Advanced Placement examinations, which are also very much a function of school atmosphere, curriculum, teaching, and student guidance. If Escalante has one lesson to bequeath us, it is that tests can function as guides to future performance, and not just as barriers to exclude the less qualified. The performance of Escalante's students might have seemed miraculous based on stereotypes. But standardized tests are blind to such biases. Through the use of cheap but reliable aptitude tests like the PSAT, jewels can be discovered that might otherwise be missed. And once such promise is uncovered, some students previously thought to be unqualified can be given an opportunity and perform successfully.

In 2006 more than a million students took over two million AP exams. This represents substantial growth over the past two decades. Yet the strong PSAT-AP relationship teaches us that a major expansion of Advanced Placement achievement remains possible in this country in all types of schools: inner city, high-performing suburbs, and just garden variety schools.

On the other hand, realism forces us to accept the fact that courses that have higher test score thresholds, such as AP Calculus, Chemistry, Physics, and Computer Science, are not going to be accessible to the majority of students, especially those in minority groups. To broaden the reach of the AP program, we must seek courses that are open to a wider audience. AP Psychology, English, and History are of this genre, as are the foreign languages, whose inclusion in school curricula not only suits a larger range of student abilities but also melds well with the current "world languages" movement in education.

It is important to note that PSAT scores predict success in AP courses *better* than do high school grades or teacher recommendations.[22] As an aid in student placement, the appendix to this chapter gives the PSAT score that yields a 50 percent probability of passing each AP exam.

Finally, the AP system is a positive influence upon which we can build improvements of our educational system. A reasonable, long-range goal for American schools is to bring up the preparatory curriculum, the teachers, and the students to the international level by increasing participation and, in the case of calculus, towards the BC examination. Rome wasn't built in a day.

As a young child John Stuart Mill complained to his father about a mathematics assignment that he had worked on unsuccessfully for an entire evening. He eventually realized that, given his mathematics knowledge at that point, there was no way he could have solved the problem. His father replied, "Unless we are asked to do the impossible we can never know the full extent of our abilities." Errors of placement surely should be more in the direction of aiming too high than too low. But they are still errors. The judicious use of aptitude tests can help us to reduce those errors substantially.

[22] Camara and Millsap 1998.

APPENDIX

PSAT SCORES AT WHICH 50% OF THE STUDENTS
SCORE 3 OR MORE ON THE AP TEST

Predicted by PSAT-Verbal		*Predicted by PSAT-Mathematics*
Spanish Literature	22.0	
Art History	36.8	
Psychology	40.3	
European History	42.4	
U.S. Government & Politics	45.2	
English Literature	45.3	
French Literature	45.6	
English Language	45.9	
French Language	45.9	
	46.0	Music
Comparative Government & Politics	46.2	
Biology	48.2	Biology
English Language	49.0	
Latin Virgil	49.0	
U.S. History	49.0	
Latin Literature	50.0	
	52.8	Microeconomics
	53.8	Macroeconomics
	55.0	Calculus BC
	56.8	Computer Science AB
	57.0	Calculus AB
	57.3	Physics B
	57.9	Chemistry
	58.8	Physics C: Mechanics
	61.4	Computer Science A
	63.2	Physics C: Electricity & Magnetism

There is no meaningful correlation between AP and PSAT in

Language: German and Spanish   Studio Art: Design and Drawing

Source: Camara 1997.

5

⁓ ⁓

Comparing the Incomparable

On the Importance of Big Assumptions
and Scant Evidence

In chapter 2, I alluded to the difficulty of obtaining comparable scores on two different achievement tests as part of the discussion of the recommendation to substitute achievement tests for aptitude tests in admissions decisions.[1] The details of equating two such tests, while important for the conclusions drawn in chapter 2, would have gotten in the way of the narrative flow. While postponing such an elaboration is acceptable, omitting it entirely is not. Now is the time.

Making fair comparisons among groups of individuals who were administered different forms of a test is a task that ranges in difficulty from easy to impossible. The more overlap there is in content between the test forms the easier the task. When they overlap completely, comparisons are straightforward; when they are completely disjoint, comparisons may be impossible. In this chapter we will focus principally on this latter situation.

This chapter developed from H. Wainer, "Comparing the Incomparable: An Essay on the Importance of Big Assumptions and Scant Evidence," *Educational Measurement: Issues and Practice* 18 (1999). 10–16.

[1] The work in this chapter was supported by the research allocation from the Educational Testing Service to the Research Statistics Group. I continue to be grateful for the opportunities that this support provides to just think. My thanks to Avi Allalouf and Stephen Sireci for encouraging comments on an earlier draft, and to Paul Holland for providing a context that helps clear thinking in this arena.

Let us begin this discussion with a common situation faced in mental testing when there are two different forms of a test being administered to two different groups of students. Such a situation might exist on two separate administrations of the SAT or the GRE; some people take it in December, some in January. Admissions officers will want scores to be comparable, but for obvious security reasons the same test items cannot be used. How can we solve this problem? We can best understand both the problem and various proposed solutions if we examine a sequence of schematic representations.

Figure 5.1 depicts the situation in which two groups are both given exactly the same test items (shading indicates that that item was given to that group). Comparisons between the groups are easy to make because the groups share a common test. If the mean score in Group I is 60 percent correct and the mean score in Group II is 30 percent, we can infer that Group I has demonstrated higher proficiency than Group II.

But let us suppose (see figure 5.2) that both groups don't get exactly the same test. Suppose we add one additional item (item $n +1$) that we give to Group I but not to Group II. Simultaneously we remove item 1 from Group I's test. Both Groups still take an n-item test. Once again we can make comparisons between Groups I and II, but we cannot be quite so sure of our conclusions.

If item 1 is much easier than item $n + 1$, Group I is at a slight disadvantage. Can we tell if this is the case? What evidence can we examine that would shed light on this possibility? If we see that examinees in Group I do much better than those in Group II on items 2 through n (what we shall call the *anchor* items), yet they do worse on item $n + 1$ than Group II does on item 1, we might infer that item 1 is easier than

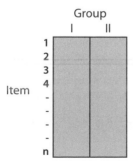

Figure 5.1. Graphical depiction of a test design in which two groups of examinees take the same form of a test

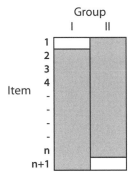

Figure 5.2. Graphical depiction of a test design in which two groups of examinees take the same form of a test except for two items

item $n + 1$. How much easier will depend on exactly how much the performance of the two groups differs on the anchor items and on the unique items. One way to estimate this is to build a model (from Group I) that predicts performance on item $n + 1$ from the anchor items, and then use that model to predict what proportion of Group II would get item $n + 1$ correct. Obviously we are assuming that a prediction model devised from one group is valid in the other. We can gather evidence supporting this assumption by building similar models within Group I that predict say, item 2 from items 3 through n, and then trying them on Group II. Since we have observed what Group II's performance on item 2 actually was, we can compare the prediction to the reality and measure the accuracy of the model. We can repeat this for all items in the anchor and summarize the accuracy thus obtained. We might also do the reverse (predict from Group II to Group I) and see how that goes. When we are all done we might choose an average prediction model from all of those developed. Such a model could be used to *equate* the two different forms of the test.

An equated test score is subjunctive; it is the score that you would have gotten had you taken a different form of the test. Whenever equating is done, there are untestable assumptions. In this instance the key assumption is that the equating model developed on the anchor test with one group will work with the other group. When the anchor test is very long with respect to that portion of the test that is unique for each group, such an assumption is weak since even a substantial violation does not yield a large effect on the estimate of the score—in the example discussed here the maximum error can only be one item.

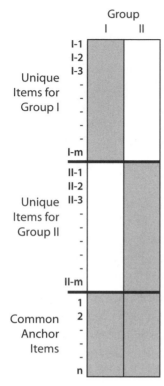

Figure 5.3. Graphical depiction of a test design in which two groups of examinees take different forms of a test with a common n-item anchor test

But having an anchor of $n - 1$ items on an n-item test is not the common situation.

Different test forms are typically employed when two groups of students are taking a test at different times and test security is an issue. In this situation there is usually a small fraction of the test that is identical for the two groups, and it is used as the equating anchor, but most of each form is unique. Such a situation is schematically depicted in figure 5.3. If n is considerably smaller than m, it is clear that the size of the untestable assumption about the performance of Group II on items I-1 through I-m becomes greater. Of course there are a number of things that can be done during test construction that can make this assumption more credible. One is to choose all items for each form randomly. If this is done, there is no reason to believe that there is any consistent difference between the two forms. A second thing that can be done is to choose the examinees that make up the two groups randomly.[2] If this is done we can be reasonably confident that the performance predicted within one group would also hold within the other.

How small can the equating anchor (n) be and still allow the different test forms to be adequately equated? On large operational tests, items are not chosen at random to build forms, but they are typically chosen to fulfill tightly constrained content and psychometric specifications. Thus it is common for n to be relatively small; for the SAT it is typically about 20 percent of the total test length (about 16–20 items on each of the two parts). It is important for the anchor section to be as small as possible commensurate with accurate equating, since it is the part of the test that will be repeated in subsequent administrations and hence at risk for security problems. But 20 percent (and at least 15–20 items) is generally considered as small as is acceptable. Because of its susceptibility to theft, the equating section is not used directly for computing an examinee's score. Also, because it is just used for equating (i.e., it is only used for aggregate purposes), its value is relatively unaffected by minor breaches in security.

But if the anchor section is shorter still, are there any methods that can yield acceptable equating? In some situations an equating section of zero length is used. Such a design is shown in figure 5.4. Can we equate when there is no anchor at all? When there are no data, we are forced to use powerful but untestable assumptions. For example, a design like that shown in figure 5.4 is used when a test is translated into another language. Group I might be examinees who take a test in English and Group II might be those who take it in Spanish. The items are, in some sense, the same for the two forms, except they have been translated; item I-1 is the English translation of II-1. Are items in translation likely to be of equal difficulty? How can we know? Obviously, knowing someone's score on one form tells us little about how the examinee would do on the other, so the term *equating* is surely a misnomer. What we hope to do is match the scales of the two forms so that the same score implies the same amount of mastery.

---

[2] This is the situation that gives validity to such procedures as equipercentile equating.

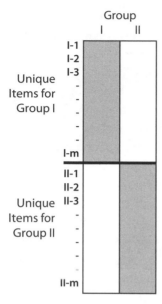

Figure 5.4. Graphical depiction of a test design in which two groups of examinees take different forms of a test with no common items

Moreover, the sort of procedure depicted in figure 5.4, relying as it does on assumptions rather than data, is sufficiently far from statistical, data-based equating, that we ought to use another word to describe it. The term *co-scaling*, denoting the placement of two tests onto the same numerical scale, but making no promises about the validity of inferences that compare one group's performance with the other's, is probably not a bad choice.

If the test items are on the same scale, then a plot of the difficulties of each item, say English versus Spanish, ought to be a straight line. But this is a necessary condition, not a sufficient one. If each item gets a fixed amount more difficult when it is translated, the two sets of difficulties will still be a diagonal line, but there is a constant effect of translation. Such an effect is inseparable from what would be observed if one group was lower in overall proficiency. By analogy, if a set of hurdles at a track meet were 10, 15, 20, 25, 30, and 35 *inches* tall, we would expect that the ease with which they could be jumped would be in the same order. But if they were "translated" to another set that were 10, 15, 20, 25, 30, and 35 *centimeters* tall (for use in Europe, say) we would expect that performance on them would fall in the same order. But there would be a higher proportion of success at each of the metric heights. We could interpret this as meaning that the Europeans were better hurdlers (and be wrong), or that the "translation" made them easier. Unless we had some athletes who participated in both track meets, there is nothing in the response data that would inform us of which was the correct interpretation. Of course this is not strictly analogous to the language translation situation since in the latter we can never assume that anyone could compete equally well on both forms.

Is co-scaling test forms without data actually done? Yes, in many situations, although which untestable assumption is made depends upon what is the purpose of the test. For example, the Educational Testing Service has a Spanish version of the SAT called the Prueba de Aptitud Academica (PAA). These two tests are placed on the same scale by assuming that the items are of the same difficulty in either language, and hence that any consistent differences observed in performance are due to differences in the abilities of the two examinee groups. Thus in 1988 when ETS researchers Bill Angoff and Linda Cook used this assumption to co-scale the PAA to the SAT, they decided that the differences they observed in performance were not due to the effect of translation on the difficulty of the items but rather that the two examinee populations were about one and a half standard deviations apart.[3]

The Canadian military, when it faced a similar problem, opted for a different untestable assumption to resolve it. Specifically, the entrance/placement test for those who want to enlist in the Canadian Military (the Canadian Forces Classification Battery; the CFCB) is offered in both English and French. Because there are comparisons that must be made among candidates who have taken different forms of this test, they must be placed on the same scale. But Canadian authorities have chosen to assume that the ability distributions of the two linguistic groups (Anglophones and Francophones) are the same.[4] Thus any differences in performance that are observed are interpreted to be due to the effects of translation. What this assumption comes down to in practice is that there are separate qualifying scores used for each form.

[3] ETS is not alone in adopting this strategy for making cross-cultural comparisons. The same assumption is made whenever the goal of an assessment is the comparison of two disparate groups (what is the alternative?). All international assessments do this (see, for example, Salganik et al. 1993).

[4] A personal communication from Commander F. T. Wilson of the Canadian Forces Personnel Applied Research Unit, March 9, 1990.

The two strategies adopted by ETS with the co-scaling of SAT and the PAA, and the Canadian military with the two linguistic forms of the CFCB, represent the two poles of what is possible. There are valid arguments supporting each position, but probably the truth lies somewhere in between in both situations. But without the possibility of gathering ancillary evidence how are we to decide how best to do it? And what sorts of ancillary evidence might there be?

Making valid comparisons without formal linkages is not impossible, but usually only if the two entities being compared are far apart. For example, in 1998 Princeton High School's football team was undefeated (they got all of the items right), whereas the Philadelphia Eagles won only three of their sixteen games (they only got 19 percent "right"). The two teams had no common opponents to allow an empirical comparison, yet is there any doubt about the outcome if they were to play one another? Theory can sometimes be quite convincing.

Are there any intermediate paths that can be taken to untie this Gordian knot? Obviously we could administer some of the items from each form to the other group, but that would tell us nothing if the traits being tested have little to do with the other language—how much do we learn about your knowledge of biology if we ask you questions on mitosis in a language you don't speak? But suppose we could find some group of examinees who speak both languages. One such design is represented in figure 5.5; Group III is the bilingual group. Such a design allows us to place all of the items on a single scale, but will it be the same scale as would have obtained for the other groups? That depends on how similar the performance of Group III is to the other two groups. Typically bilinguals are not like monolinguals in many important ways, but still it does provide some evidence.[5]

Another alternative might be to make up some nonlinguistic items that could be administered to everyone and hence serve as an anchor, but would the relationship between that anchor and the rest of the test be strong enough to allow the kinds of inferences needed? Such an approach can give some help, but usually not enough for serious purposes. Indeed, if a nonlinguistic test allows us to adequately connect two linguistic forms, why do we need the latter?

[5] See Sireci 1997 for further discussion of this methodology.

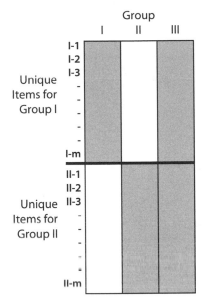

Figure 5.5. Graphical depiction of a test design in which two groups of examinees take different forms of a test with no common items, but a third group takes both forms.

The usual method for placing two tests onto a common scale involves the idea of random assignment of either items to tests or examinees to groups. We do this because with random assignment of items to test forms we have strong a priori evidence to believe that the tests thus formed are of equal difficulty (the SAT-PAA model). With random assignment of examinees to groups we have strong a priori evidence to believe that the two groups' abilities are the same (the Canadian military model). But the further away the assignment rule is from random the weaker is the evidence. In the current problem anything approaching random assignment is impossible. Are there any other alternatives that might be explored?

An intermediate path was explored by Israel's National Institute for Testing and Evaluation (NITE).[6] NITE produces a test called the Psychometric Entrance Test (PET) that is an important component in admissions decisions to Israeli universities. The PET is offered in many languages including (but not limited to) Hebrew, Arabic, English, Russian, Spanish, and French. Scores are compared across these various translations. The NITE staff is convinced that the Canadian assumption

---

[6] Beller, Gafni, and Hanani 2005.

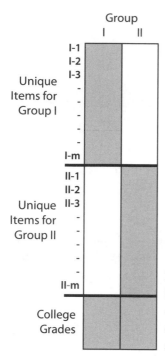

Figure 5.6. Graphical depiction of a test design in which two groups of examinees take different forms of a test with no common items with a common ancillary measure that may be used as an anchor test.

is untenable; the population of examinees who take the test in Russian is very different from those who take it in Arabic, for example. But NITE also believes that the ETS assumption (that there is no difference in scores due to translation) is also not correct. But they do have ancillary evidence that is directly related to the key latent dimensions of the test—the performance of some of the examinees in college. Thus the Israeli situation can be represented as in figure 5.6. Of course this doesn't completely solve the problem since there are nonrandomly missing data; how would students who didn't attend college have done? Moreover, students take different courses in college and so their grades represent a nonuniform scoring system. Yet it is something, and it allows a check on what otherwise would be entirely untestable assumptions to place the various linguistic forms of the PET onto a common scale.

NITE uses the criterion data, college grades, to test assumptions about the effects of translation on item difficulty. Initially they used the ETS assumption that item I-1 has the same difficulty as item II-1, I-2 is the same as II-2, and so on. But when they found that one group's superior performance on their version of the PET did not yield analogous

When considering the technical details associated with this approach to equating, one arrives, almost by surprise, at an innovative method for test scoring. My colleague Charles Lewis has named it validity-based scoring (VBS). The key idea is to use the pattern of responses on the test to predict what the examinee's performance would be on the validity criterion of interest, and that predicted value becomes the examinee's score on the test. Each form of the test might have its own prediction equation, but all examinees would then have a score on the same scale. This has a number of remarkable benefits. Four of them are the following:

1. You cannot score a test without gathering validity data.
2. Examinees' scores vary depending on the prospective use of the tests
3. If a test is being used for an invalid purpose all examinees will have the same score.
4. Different forms are automatically placed on the same scale (the scale of the criterion).

superior performance in college grades, they questioned the validity of that assumption. The result of that questioning was a further adjustment of the PET scores that used the college grades as an equating anchor.

This brings me to the point of this chapter. Placing the scores of two tests that are given to two disparate groups onto a common scale requires an untestable assumption: perhaps an assumption about their relative mean abilities, perhaps about the relative difficulties of the items, perhaps a mixture of both. There are no statistical methods that can come to the rescue. In the case of test forms translated into different languages, we can try to make the untestable assumption as plausible as possible through care in translation and form preparation. In the SAT-PAA situation, half the items originated in Spanish and were translated into English; the other half were prepared in the reverse order. Care was taken to assure that the item difficulties were in the same order on both forms. Such care reduces the possibility of certain kinds of biases, but does not eliminate them. Remember my earlier example of hurdles in centimeters and inches. Following the same preparation rules would not affect the overall bias; indeed a plot of the item difficulties of one form against those of the other would show that the items lined up perfectly.

There are many statistical schemes that purport to allow us to co-scale two tests administered on different populations[7] but hidden away in all of them is one of the two untestable assumptions we have described here; either characterizing the structure of the item difficulties across populations (usually equal) or the populations' abilities. Without additional data there is no alternative to such untestable assumptions.

Of course which assumption is made is determined by the inferences we wish to make from the test. For example if we wish to compare the abilities of two populations (e.g., Spanish vs. English in the SAT/PAA situation) we must assume that the items maintain their same difficulty. If instead, we assume that all differences in performance are due to the effects of translation, the point of our investigation is mooted. Thus we infer that the principal purpose of the Canadian military testing program is to make comparisons within language groups; for surely between-group comparisons are strongly affected by the identifying assumption of equality.

The Israeli college admissions program provides one example of a situation in which there is a need for between-group comparisons and there are ancillary data to aid in making them. I suspect that this is always likely to be the case—if there are no ancillary data, there probably is no need to place them on a common scale.

How plausible are these two different kinds of identifying assumptions? The idea that the difficulty of a carefully translated item does not change radically is a compelling one, especially compelling if you must make cross group comparisons. But how likely is it? For some subjects that are, in their essence, nonverbal (e.g., mathematics) such an assumption may not be far-fetched. But for items whose essence is verbal it would seem unlikely. Michal Beller and her colleagues at NITE[8] provide an extended discussion of this issue. They give a compelling example of the problem within the testing of analytical reasoning:

---

[7] Angoff 1972; Angoff and Modu 1973; Angoff and Cook 1988; Hambleton 1993; Poortinga and van de Vijver 1991; Sireci, Bastari, and Allalouf 1998; van de Vijver and Poortinga 1997.

[8] Beller, Gafni, and Hanani 2005.

In an attempt to preserve the precise structure of the original logic items in the translated version (for example, preserving negatives, double negatives, conjunctions such as "only," "also" etc.), it is sometimes necessary to change the structure so that the syntax of the target language will be correct. For example, the syntax of the Hebrew structure *"all p's are not q"* is ambiguous in English. Thus, a statement in Hebrew such as: <u>All</u> *birds of prey are* <u>*not*</u> *green* (meaning that there is not even one bird of prey that is green) cannot be directly translated into English. In order to preserve the exact Hebrew meaning the structure of the English sentence has to be changed as follows: <u>No</u> *birds of prey are green.* A similar difficulty arises when this sentence has to be translated into French. In French, "all" cannot be followed by a negative. Therefore, the translation has to be: *Aucun oiseau prédateur n'est vert.*

The complexity of decoding the Hebrew version *"All birds of prey are* <u>*not*</u> *green"* surely seems greater than that required for the English version *"*<u>*No*</u> *birds of prey are green."* What are the limits of accuracy of inferences made under the assumption that they are of equal difficulty?

There is no surefire solution to the problem of making comparisons among groups in which there are no common elements. All solutions must include at least one untestable assumption. However, we can make an advance if we formalize the estimation problem within the context of a mathematical model of appropriate form and complexity. Recent advances in estimation methods have made practical embedding complex models into a fully Bayesian framework. This approach has yielded fruit in many and varied situations.[9] Such modeling cannot work miracles, but it can provide us with three important benefits:

1. By embedding the problem within the context of a formal statistical model we must be explicit about our assumptions.
2. Through the use of sensitivity studies we can assess the stability of our inferences to various levels of violation of the assumptions.

[9] See Gelman et al. 1995, for a thorough description of such methods and Bradlow, Wainer, and Wang 1999 for an example of how such models can be applied within the context of modern test theory.

3. Through the appropriate inclusion of parameters for ancillary information in the model, we can optimally weight any such information that might become available. It will also allow us to determine the value of such information that might become available.[10]

Now that the foundation has been laid, we can return to the problem that motivated this discussion, substituting achievement tests or aptitude tests for college admission. The model shown in figure 5.3 is the one currently used for co-scaling two different science achievement tests (say physics and chemistry). The common link is the SAT-Math. We have seen in chapter 4 how well math aptitude, as measured by the SAT or the PSAT, can predict achievement scores for the various sciences, and so placing such tests on a common scale with this kind of common link is credible. It still faces some logical issues, but this is a plausible solution to a very difficult problem. But if the SAT is no longer required, this link disappears.

Thus the irony is that using such achievement test scores for admission is only possible if the aptitude test is also required, but if it is not, the value of the achievement tests for this purpose disappears with it.

In the same way the SAT-Verbal test is used as an anchor for co-scaling achievement tests in the humanities and the social sciences. It works passably for some areas (e.g., History and English) but not others (e.g., Spanish).

But there remains no credible way to make comparisons among applicants who present achievement test scores in different foreign languages. And, of course, we still cannot resolve the issues dealing with

[10] The sorts of information I envisage here would be criterion data as in the Israeli example, or results obtained from bilinguals, of both kinds, who take both forms of the test.

This is the wrong forum for the development of such a model, for my goal in writing this chapter was to explicate the character of the problem. But a reasonable way to think about the model is to imagine that the variation in performance between two groups is a variance that can be decomposed into two components. One component is the difference between the means of the two ability distributions, and the other is the difference in the item difficulties due to the effects of translation. The untestable assumption provides weights for these two components. The ETS/PAA solution uses weights of 1 and 0; the Canadian solution uses weights of 0 and 1. It is more likely (depending on test and examinee groups) that less extreme values are correct. Ancillary information must be used to estimate such weights.

comparisons between a science score and one in the humanities. There is no common link that will help us answer the motivating question "Was Mozart a better composer than Einstein was a physicist?"

AN OBITER DICTUM

It is generally considered good practice that, when we are faced with a situation in which our inferences rely heavily on untestable assumptions, we proceed very cautiously indeed. Ancillary evidence takes on much greater importance in these situations than it does when assumptions can be tested directly. The sorts of ancillary evidence I refer to may be logical or empirical. One example of the latter are the college performance data that are used to fine-tune the calibration of Israel's PET. This is surely the case for groups that are separated by language and culture, but let us think a little more broadly.

Suppose we have a design like that shown in figure 5.6 and have made the assumption that an item maintains the same difficulty when it is given to different groups. Few would disagree that we ought to question the assumption of homogeneous difficulty if we find consistent differences in performance on the criterion (college grades) that are not matched by differences in performance on the different forms of the entrance test. Now let us suppose that Group I consists of males and Group II consists of females. Tests are never equated by sex. Clearly there is no design that would allow such an equating except through a common criterion. Yet when we use college grades as a common criterion[11] we find the same kinds of consistent differences that led the Israelis to adjust PET scores. Of course there are other possible explanations (e.g., college grades reflect abilities unmeasured by college entrance test scores), but it seems disingenuous to dismiss one of the possible explanations, where if the groups were defined differently (e.g., by language or ethnicity) it would be the first assumption questioned.

Note that the adoption of the Canadian military model, which resolves the lack of identifiability by assuming identical ability distributions, would yield different cut-scores by sex. Such an approach, as

---

[11] In math see Wainer and Steinberg 1992.

justifiable statistically as the current approach, would eliminate in a stroke all sex differences in the awarding of scholarships by test score. Using validity-based scoring would also help, although it may take some doing to gain agreement on suitable criteria. Current legal restrictions limit what can be done in this regard, but perhaps laws and regulations can be changed if sufficient evidence can be provided.

Of course one can sensibly argue that the physical and cultural differences that characterize men and women are not analogous to the differences that characterize different language groups. But the seriousness of the test's consequences as well as the reliability of the ancillary validity information suggests that we ought to consider explicitly the unstated assumptions about the equivalence of test forms under such circumstances. Indeed, one goal of this chapter is to instigate broader thinking about the inferences we draw from test data by making explicit some of the assumptions that often underlie those inferences.

6

⚬⚬ ⚬⚬

On Examinee Choice
in Educational Testing

If you allow choice, you will regret it; if you don't
allow choice, you will regret it; whether you allow
choice or not, you will regret both.
—Søren Kierkegaard 1986, 24

In chapters 2 and 5 we explored the difficulties encountered in making comparisons among candidates when the candidates themselves
are the ones who decide which aspects of their experience and ability to present. The difficulties in making such comparisons fairly can
be overwhelming. Let us now consider the more limited situation that
manifests itself when the examination scores of students who are to
be compared are obtained from test items that the students have chosen themselves. Such a situation occurred often in the beginning of
the twentieth century, but gradually fell out of favor as evidence accumulated that highlighted the shortcomings of such "build it yourself"
exams. But the lessons learned seem to have been forgotten, and there is
renewed hope that examinee choice can improve measurement, partic-
ularly when assessing what are called *generative* or *constructive processes*
in learning. To be able to measure such processes, directors of testing
programs believe they must incorporate items that require examinees to respond freely (what, in testing jargon, are called "constructed

This chapter developed from H. Wainer and D. Thissen, "On Examinee Choice in
Educational Testing," *Review of Educational Research*, 64 (1994): 159–195.

response" items) into their previously highly constrained (multiple choice) standardized exams.

It is hoped that items that require lengthy responses, such as essays, mathematical proofs, experiments, portfolios of work, or other performance-based tasks are better measures of deep understanding, broad analysis, and higher levels of performance than responses to traditional multiple-choice items. Examples of tests currently using constructed response items are the College Board's Advanced Placement examinations in United States History, European History, United States Government and Politics, Physics, Calculus, and Chemistry. There are many others.

Multiple-choice items are small and take only a modest amount of time to answer. Thus a one-hour exam can easily contain forty to fifty such items. Each item contributes only a small amount to the examinee's final score. This has two important benefits. First, it allows the test developer to provide a reasonable representation of the content of the area being examined. And second, examinees are not affected too severely if a question or two represent material that was not covered by their particular course.

But when an exam consists, in whole or in part, of constructed response items, this is no longer true. Constructed response items like essays take a much longer time to answer, and so the test developer must face unfortunate options:

1. Use only a small number of such items, thus limiting the coverage of the domain of the test.
2. Increase the length of time it takes to administer the exam; this is usually impractical.
3. Confine the test questions to a core curriculum that all valid courses ought to cover. This option may discourage teachers from broadening their courses beyond that core.

To try to resolve this difficult situation it is common practice to provide a pool of questions and to allow each examinee to choose a subset of them to answer.

But what are we estimating when we allow choice? When a test is given, we ordinarily estimate a score that represents the examinee's proficiency. The usual estimate of proficiency is based on estimated performance from a sample drawn from the entire distribution of possible items. Most practitioners I have spoken to who favor allowing choice, argue that choice provides the opportunity for the examinees to show themselves to best advantage. However, this is only true if examinees choose the item that would give them the highest score.

Unfortunately, choice items are typically not of equal difficulty, despite the best efforts of test builders to make them so. This fact, combined with the common practice of not adjusting the credit given to mirror the differences in item difficulty, yields the inescapable conclusion that it matters what choice an examinee makes. Examinees who chose the more difficult question will, on average, get lower scores than if they had chosen the easier item. The observation that all examinees do not choose those items that will show their proficiency to best advantage completes this unhappy syllogism.

Even in the absence of attractive alternatives, is allowing examinee choice a sensible strategy? Under what conditions can we allow choice without compromising the fairness and quality of the test? I will not provide a complete answer to these questions. I will, however, illustrate some of the pitfalls associated with allowing examinee choice; provide a vocabulary and framework that aids in the clear discussion of the topic; outline some experimental steps that can tell us whether choice can be implemented fairly; and provide some experimental evidence that illuminates the topic.

Let us begin with a brief history of examinee choice in testing, in the belief that it is easier to learn from the experiences of our clever predecessors than to try to relive those experiences.

A SELECTIVE HISTORY OF CHOICE IN EXAMS

I shall confine my attention to some college entrance exams used during the first half of the twentieth century in the United States. The College Entrance Examination Board (CEEB) began testing prospective college students at the juncture of the nineteen and twentieth centuries. By 1905 exams were offered in thirteen subjects: English, French, German, Greek, Latin, Spanish, Mathematics, Botany, Chemistry, Physics,

Drawing, Geography, and History.[1] Most of these exams contained some degree of choice. In addition, all of the science exams used portfolio assessment, as it might be called in modern terminology. For example, on the 1905 Botany exam 37 percent of the score was based on the examinee's laboratory notebook. The remaining 63 percent was based on a ten-item exam. Examinees were asked to answer seven of those ten items, which yielded the possibility of 120 different unique examinee-created "forms."

The computation of the number of choice-created forms is further complicated by some remarkably vague exam questions.[2] Question 10 from the 1905 Botany exam illustrates this profound lack of specificity:[3]

10. Select some botanical topic not included in the questions above, and write a brief exposition of it.

The Chemistry and Physics exams shared the structure of the Botany exam.

As the CEEB grew more experienced, the structure of its tests changed. The portfolio aspect disappeared by 1913, when the requirement of a teacher's certification that the student had, in fact, completed a lab course was substituted for the student's notebook. By 1921 this certification was no longer required.

The extent to which examinees were permitted choice varied; see table 6.1, in which the number of possible examinee-created "forms" is listed for four subjects over thirty-five years. The contrast between the flamboyance of the English exam and the staid German exam is instructive. Only once, in 1925, was any choice allowed on the German exam ("Answer only *one* of the following six questions"). The lack of choice seen in the German exam is representative of all of the foreign language exams except Latin. The amount of choice seen in Physics and Chemistry parallel that for most exams that allowed choice. The English exam between 1913 and 1925 is unique in terms of the possible variation.[4] No

---

[1] College Entrance Examination Board 1905.

[2] Indeed it challenges the very nature of what we would call a standardized test.

[3] The graders for each test were identified, with their institutional affiliations. A practice, if followed in these litigious times, that would make finding people willing to grade exams a task of insuperable difficulty.

[4] Section II of the 1921 exam asked the examinee to answer five of twenty-six questions. This alone yielded more than 65,000 different possible "forms." When coupled with

TABLE 6.1
Number of Possible Test Forms Generated
by Examinee Choice Patterns

	Subject			
Year	Chemistry	Physics	English	German
1905	54	81	64	1
1909	18	108	60	1
1913	8	144	7,260	1
1917	252	1,620	1,587,600	1
1921	252	216	2,960,100	1
1925	126	56	48	6
1929	20	56	90	1
1933	20	10	24	1
1937	15	2	1	1
1941	1	1	1	1

equating of these examinee-constructed forms for possible differential difficulty was considered.

By 1941 the CEEB offered fourteen exams, but only three (American History, Contemporary Civilization, and Latin) allowed examinee choice. Even among these, choice was sharply limited:

- In the American History exam there were six essay questions. Essays 1, 2, and 6 were mandatory. There were three questions about the American Constitution (labeled 3A, 4A, and 5A) as well as three parallel questions about the British constitution (3B, 4B and 5B). The examinee could choose either the A questions or the B questions.
- In the Contemporary Civilization exam there were six essay questions. Questions 1–4 and 6 were all mandatory. Question 5 consisted of six short-answer items out of which the examinee had to answer five.
- The Latin exam had many parts. In sections requiring translation from Latin to English or vice versa, the examinee often had the opportunity to pick one passage from a pair to translate.

Section III (pick one essay topic from among fifteen) and Section I ("answer 1 of the following 3") we arrive at the unlikely figure shown in table 6.1.

In 1942, the last year of the program, there were fewer exams given; none allowed examinee choice. Why did the use of choice disappear over the forty years of this pioneering examination program? My investigations did not yield a definitive answer, although many hints suggest that issues of fairness propelled the CEEB toward the test structure on which it eventually settled. My insight into this history was sharpened during the reading of Carl Brigham's remarkable 1934 report on "the first major attack on the problem of grading the written examination."[5] This exam required the writing of four essays. There were six topics; 1 and 6 were required of all examinees and there was a choice offered between topics 2 and 3 and between topics 4 and 5. The practice of allowing examinee choice was termed "alternative questions."

As Brigham noted,

> When alternative questions are used, different examinations are in fact set for the various groups electing the different patterns. The total score reported to the college is to a certain extent a sum of the separate elements, and the manner in which the elements combine depends on their intercorrelation. This subject is too complex to be investigated with this material.

Brigham's judgment of the difficulty is mirrored by Princeton psychometrician Harold Gulliksen, who, in his classic 1950 text wrote, "In general it is impossible to determine the appropriate adjustment without an inordinate amount of effort. Alternative questions should always be avoided."

Both of these comments suggest that while adjusting for the effects of examinee choice is possible, it is too difficult to do within an operational context. I suspect that even these careful researchers underestimated the difficulty of satisfactorily accomplishing such an adjustment.[6] This view was supported by legendary psychometrician Ledyard Tucker (1910–2004),[7] who said, "I don't think that they knew how to deal with choice then. I'm not sure we know how now."

---

[5] Carl Brigham (1890–1943) was, arguably, the inventor of the SAT.

[6] Their warnings are strongly reminiscent of Fermat's marginal comments about his only recently proved theorem.

[7] Personal communication, February 10, 1993.

The core of the problem of choice is that when it is allowed, the examinees' choices generate what can be thought of as different forms of the test. These forms may not be of equal difficulty. When different forms are administered, standards of good testing practice require that those forms be statistically equated so that individuals who took different forms can be compared fairly. Perhaps, through pretesting and careful test construction, it may be possible to make the differences in form difficulty sufficiently small that further equating is not required. An unbiased estimate of the difficulty of any item can not be obtained from a self-selected sample of the examinee population. The CEEB made no attempt to avoid such a sample. Perhaps that is why Brigham said, "This subject is too complex to be investigated with this material."

ARE CHOICE ITEMS OF EQUAL DIFFICULTY?

When choice items are prepared, item writers strive to make them of equal difficulty. But this is a task that seems to be beyond current test construction methods. Until recently, evidence about the relative difficulty of such items was suggestive, but equivocal. Let me illustrate this point with three simple examples. The first and the second come from operational testing programs and the third from a special data-gathering effort.

Example 1: 1968 AP Chemistry Test
Shown in table 6.2 are results[8] for a form of the College Board's Advanced Placement chemistry test. One group of examinees chose to take problem 4 and a second group chose problem 5. While their scores on the common multiple-choice section were about the same (11.7 vs. 11.2 out of a possible 25), their scores on the choice problem were very different (8.2 vs. 2.7 on a ten-point scale). There are several possible conclusions to be drawn from this. Four among them are the following:

1. Problem 5 is a good deal more difficult than problem 4.
2. Small differences in performance on the multiple-choice section translate into much larger differences on the free response questions.

[8] Reported by Fremer, Jackson and McPeek (1968).

TABLE 6.2
Average Scores on AP Chemistry 1968

Choice group	Multiple choice section	Choice problem	
		4	5
1	11.7	8.2	
2	11.2		2.7

3. The proficiency required to do the two problems is not strongly related to that required to do well on the multiple-choice section.
4. Item 5 is selected by those who are less likely to do well on it.

Investigation of the content of the questions as well as studies of the dimensionality of the entire test suggest that conclusion (1) is the most credible. This interpretation would suggest that scores on these two examinee-created test forms ought to have been equated. They were not.

Example 2: 1988 AP United States History Test
The first example indicated that those who chose the more difficult problem were placed at a disadvantage. In this example I identify more specifically the examinees who tended to choose more difficult items. Consider the results shown in figure 6.1 from the 1988 administration of the College Board's Advanced Placement test in United States history. This test comprises 100 multiple-choice items and two essays. Essay 1 is mandatory; the second is chosen by the examinee from among five topics (2–6). Shown in figure 6.1 are the average scores given for each of those topics, as well as the proportion of men and women who chose it.

Topic 3 had the lowest average scores for both men and women. The usual interpretation of this finding is that topic 3 was the most difficult. This topic was about twice as popular among women as among men. An alternative interpretation of these findings might be that the lowest proficiency examinees chose this topic, and that a greater proportion of women than men fell into this category. This illustrates again how any finding within a self-selected sample yields ambiguous interpretations.

Similar studies with similar findings have been carried out on all of the AP tests that allow choice.[9] There are also substantial sex and ethnic

[9] Pomplun et al. 1991; DeMauro 1991.

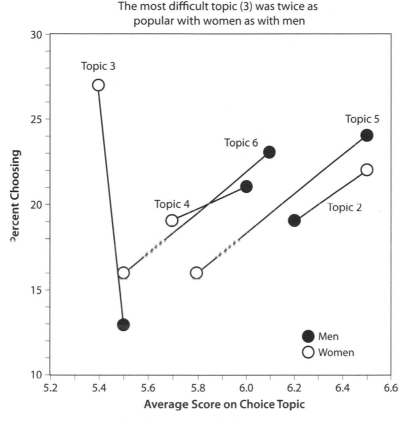

Figure 6.1. Scores on the choice essays for the 1988 AP United States History test for men and women examinees

differences in choice on third-, fifth-, and eighth-grade passage-based reading comprehension tests.[10] The phenomenon of students choosing poorly is so widespread that evidence of it occurs wherever one looks. In one description of the effect of choice on a test of basic writing, the investigators found that the more that examinees liked a particular topic, the lower they scored on an essay they subsequently wrote on that topic![11]

Although test developers try to make up choice questions that are of equivalent difficulty, they are rarely successful. Of course this con-

[10] Fitzpatrick and Yen 1993.
[11] Powers et al. 1992.

clusion is clouded by possible alternative explanations that have their origin in self-selection: for example, the choice items are not unequally difficult, but rather the people who choose them are unequally proficient. So long as there is self-selection, this alternative cannot be completely dismissed, although it can be discredited through the use of additional information. If it can be shown that choice items are not of equal difficulty, it follows that some individuals will be placed at a disadvantage by their choice of item—they choose to take a test some of whose items are more difficult than those on a corresponding test for other examinees—at least to the extent that this extra difficulty is not adjusted away in the scoring.

Example 3: The Only Unambiguous Data on Choice and Difficulty

In a special data-gathering effort, we repeatedly presented examinees with a choice between two items, but then required them to answer both.[12] One aspect of the results appears in table 6.3. The column labeled "Item difficulty" contains the percentage of students nationally who answered that item correctly.[13] We see that even though item 12 was much more difficult than item 11, there were still some students who chose it.

Perhaps the examinees who chose item 12 did so because they had some special knowledge that made this item less difficult for them than item 11. Table 6.4 shows the performance of examinees on each of these items broken down by the items they chose. Note that 11 percent of those examinees who chose item 12 responded correctly, whereas 69 percent of them answered item 11 correctly. Moreover, this group performed more poorly on both of the items than examinees who chose item 11. The obvious implication drawn from this example is that examinees do not always choose wisely, and that less proficient examinees exacerbate matters through their unfortunate choices. Data from the rest of this experiment consistently supported these conclusions.

The conclusion drawn from many results like this is that as examinees' ability increases they tend to choose more wisely—they know enough to be able to determine which choices are likely to be the least difficult. The other side of this is as ability declines choice becomes

---

[12] Wang, Wainer, and Thissen 1993.
[13] An operational administration of these items involving more than 18,000 examinees.

TABLE 6.3
The Difficulty and Popularity of Two Choice Items

Item chosen	Number choosing	Item difficulty
11	180	82%
12	45	22%

TABLE 6.4
The Proportion of Students Getting Each Item Correct Based
on Item Selected

	Item chosen	
Item answered	11	12
11	0.84	0.69
12	0.23	0.11

closer and closer to random. What this means is that, on average, lower-ability students, when given choice, are more likely to choose more difficult items than their competitors at the higher end of the proficiency scale. Thus allowing choice will tend to exacerbate group differences.

STRATEGIES FOR FAIR TESTING
WHEN CHOICE IS ALLOWED

I will now examine two alternative strategies for achieving the primary goal of examinee choice: to provide the opportunity for examinees to show themselves to the best advantage. The first is to aid students in making wiser choices; the second is to diminish the unintended consequences of a poor choice through statistical equating of the choice items.

What Are the Alternative Strategies?

There appear to be two paths that can be followed: eliciting wiser choices by examinees or equating test forms. The second option removes the necessity for the first; in fact it makes examinee choice unnecessary.

How can we improve examinees' judgment about which items to select? I fear that this can be done optimally only by asking examinees to answer all items, and then scoring just those responses that yield the highest estimate of performance. This strategy is not without its drawbacks. First, it takes more testing time, and choice is often instituted to keep testing time within practical limits. Second, many examinees, upon hearing that "only one of the six items will be counted" will only answer one. Thus, this strategy may commingle measures of grit, choice-wisdom, and risk aversion with those of proficiency. It also adds in a positive bias associated with luck.

A more practical approach might be to try to improve the instructions to the examinees about how the test is to be graded, so as to help them make better choices. Perhaps it would help if the instructions about choice made it clear that there is no advantage to answering a hard item correctly relative to answering an easy one, if such is indeed the case. Current instructions do not address this issue. For example, the instructions about choice on the 1989 AP Chemistry test, reproduced in their entirety are,

Solve ONE of the two problems in this part. (A second problem will not be scored).

Contrast this with the care that is taken to instruct examinees about the hazards of guessing. These are taken from the same test:

Many candidates wonder whether or not to guess the answers to questions about which they are not certain. In this section of the examination, as a correction for haphazard guessing, one-fourth of the number of questions you answer incorrectly will be subtracted from the number you answer correctly. It is improbable, therefore, that mere guessing will improve your score significantly; it may even lower your score, and it does take time. If however, you are not sure of the correct answer but have some knowledge of the question and are able to eliminate one or more of the answer choices as wrong, your chance of getting the right answer is improved, and it may be to your advantage to answer such a question.

Perhaps with better instructions the quality of examinee choices can be improved. At the moment there is no evidence supporting the conjecture that they can be, or if so, by how much. An experimental test of the value of improved instructions could involve one randomly selected group with the traditional instructions and another with a more informative set. We could then see which group has higher average scores on the choice section.

I am not confident that this option solves the problem of making exams that allow choice fairer. To do so requires reducing the impact of unwise choice. This could be accomplished by adjusting the scores on the choice items statistically for their differential difficulty: the process called *equating* that we have already discussed.

How Does Equating Affect the Examinee's Task?

Equating appears, at first blush, to make the examinee's task of choosing more difficult still. If no equating is done the instructions to the examinee should be

Answer that item which seems easiest to you.

We hope that the examinees choose correctly, but we will not know if they do not. If we equate the choice items (give more credit for harder items than easier ones), the instructions should be

Pick that item which, after we adjust, will give you the highest score.

This task could be akin to the problem faced by competitive divers, who choose their routine of dives from within various homogeneous groups of dives. The diver's decision is informed by several factors:

- Knowledge of the "degree of difficulty" of each dive
- Knowledge of the concatenation rule by which the dive's difficulty and the diver's performance rating are combined (they are multiplied)
- Knowledge, obtained through long practice, of what his or her score is likely to be on all of the dives

Armed with this knowledge, the diver can select a set of dives that is most likely to maximize his or her total score.

The diver's scenario is one in which an individual's informed choice provides a total score that seems to be close enough to optimal for useful purposes. Is a similar scenario possible within the plausible confines of standardized testing? Let us examine the aspects of required knowledge point by point.

Specifying how much each item will count in advance is possible, either by calculating the empirical characteristics of each item from pretest data or, as is currently the case, by specifying how much each one counts by fiat. I favor the former, because it allows each item to contribute to total score in a way that minimizes measurement error. An improvident choice of a priori weights can have a serious deleterious effect on measurement accuracy.[14]

Specifying the concatenation rule (how examinee performance and item characteristics interact to contribute to the examinee's score) in advance is also possible, but may be quite complex. Perhaps a rough approximation can be worked out, or perhaps one could present a graphical solution, but for now this remains a question. The difficulties that we might have with specifying the concatenation rule are largely technical, and workable solutions could probably be developed.

A much more formidable obstacle is providing the examinees with enough information so that they can make wise choices. This seems completely out of reach, for even if examinees know how much a particular item will, if answered correctly, contribute to their final score, it does no good unless the examinees have a good idea of their likelihood of answering the item correctly. The extent to which such knowledge is imperfect would then correspond to the difference between the score that is obtained and the optimal score that could have been obtained with a perfect choice. The nature of security associated with modern large-scale testing makes impossible the sort of rehearsal that provides divers with accurate estimates of their performance under various choice options.

The prospect appears bleak for simultaneously allowing choice and satisfying the canons of good practice that require the equating of test forms of unequal difficulty. The task that examinees face in choosing

---

[14] Lukhele, Thissen, and Wainer 1994; Wainer and Thissen 1993.

items when they are adjusted seems too difficult. But is it? There remain two glimmers of hope:

1. Equating the choice items before scoring them
2. Declaring that the choice is part of the item, and so if you choose unwisely, tough

Option 1, the equating of the various choice forms, seems better. If we can do this, the examinees should be indifferent about which items they answer, because successful equating means that an examinee will receive, in expectation, the same score regardless of the form administered. This is happy, but ironic, news; for it appears that we can allow choice and have fair tests only when choice is unnecessary. To answer the question posed at the beginning of this section: When we do not equate selected items, the problem of choice faced by the examinee can be both difficult and important. When we do equate the items, the selection problem simultaneously becomes much more difficult but considerably less important.

Equating choice items involves arranging each item to be answered by a randomly selected subset of the population. For example, if we had a section with three items and we wanted examinees to choose two of them to answer, we would need to assign one randomly selected third of the examinees to answer item 1 and allow them to choose between items 2 and 3. A second group would be assigned item 2 and be allowed to choose between 1 and 3; and the last group would have to answer item 3 and get to choose between 1 and 2. In this way we can obtain unbiased estimates of the difficulties of all three items and the examinees would still have some choice. I will not go further into the more technical details of how to equate choice items, as that discussion is beyond the scope of this chapter.

Option 2, making the choice part of the item, is an interesting possibility and I will devote all of chapter 7 to its exploration.

What Can We Learn from Choice Behavior?

Thus far, my proposed requirements prior to implementing examinee choice fairly require a good deal of work on the part of both the examinee and the examiner. I am aware that extra work and expense are not part of the plan for many choice tests. Often choice is allowed because there are too many plausible items to be asked and too little time to answer them. Is all of this work really necessary? Almost surely. At a minimum one cannot know whether it is necessary unless it is done. To paraphrase Derek Bok's comment on the cost of education, if you think doing it right is expensive, try doing it wrong. Yet many well-meaning and otherwise clear-thinking individuals ardently support choice in exams. Why? The answer to this question must, perforce, be impressionistic. I have heard a variety of reasons. Some are nonscientific; one, from educational researcher Karen Scheingold was "To show the examinees that we care." The implication is that by allowing choice we are giving examinees the opportunity to do their best. I find this justification difficult to accept, because there is overwhelming evidence to indicate that this goal is unlikely to be accomplished. Which is more important, fairness, or the appearance of fairness? Ordinarily the two go together, but when they do not, we must be fair, and do our best to explain why.

DISCUSSION

So far I have painted a bleak psychometric picture for the use of examinee choice within fair tests. To make tests with choice fair requires equating the test forms generated by the choice for their differential difficulty. Accomplishing this requires either some special data-gathering effort or trust in assumptions about the unobserved responses that, if true, obviate the need for choice. If we can successfully equate choice items, we have thus removed the value of choice in any but the most superficial sense.

Thus far I have confined the discussion to situations in which it is reasonable to assign any of the choice items to any examinee. Such an assumption underlies the notions of equating. I will call situations in which examinees are given such a choice *small choice*.

Small Choice

Small choice is used most commonly because test designers believe that measurement of the underlying construct may be contaminated by the particular context in which the material is embedded. It is sometimes thought that a purer estimate of the underlying construct may be obtained by allowing examinee choice from among several different contexts. Consider, for example the following two versions of the same math problem:

1. The distance between the Earth and the Sun is 93 million miles. If a rocket ship took 40 days to make the trip, what was its average speed?
2. The Kentucky Derby is one and one-fourth miles in length. When Northern Dancer won the race with a time of 2 minutes, what was his average speed?

The answer to both problems may be expressed in miles per hour. Both problems are formally identical, except for differences in the difficulty of the arithmetic. Allowing an examinee to choose between these items might allow us to test the construct of interest (Does the student know the relation Rate × Time = Distance?), while at the same time letting the examinees pick the context within which they feel more comfortable.

The evidence available so far tells us that with enough preparatory work small choice can be implemented on exams fairly. But if this option is followed carefully the reasons for allowing choice have been mooted.

But What about Big Choice?

It was late at night in a dimly lit chamber hidden in the bowels of the admissions office of Ivy University. Through bleary eyes, Samantha Stewart, the admissions director, was reviewing the pile of dossiers that represented the entering class of 2014. Almost all of the tough decisions had been made. But one remained that she alone must deal with. There was but a single opening with two worthy competitors for that very last spot. Both applicants had taken a rigorous program of study in high school and both excelled. Their SAT scores were nearly identical and their letters of recommendation could not have been better. One student was first violin in the all-state orchestra and the other was first-string quarterback on the all-state football team. Either would make a fine addition to the class, but there was only room for one. How was the director to decide? She was

faced with trying to answer a seemingly impossible question: Was student
A a better violinist than student B was a quarterback?

So far we have focused on small choice, in which we could plausibly
ask individuals to answer any of the options available. We concluded
that small choice is possible to do fairly, but only with a substantial
amount of preparation. What about big choice, illustrated in the previous example? This is a much more difficult problem. Can we find an
evidence-based solution?

Throughout the educational process decisions are made using nonrandomly selected data. Admissions to college are decided among individuals whose dossiers contain mixtures of material; one high school
student may opt to emphasize courses in math and science, whereas
another may have taken advanced courses in French and Spanish. One
student might have been editor of the school newspaper, another captain of the football team, and yet a third might have been first violin in
the orchestra. All represent commitment and success; how are they to
be compared? Is your French better than my calculus? Is such a comparison sensible? Admissions offices at competitive universities face
these problems all the time; dismissing them is being blind to reality.
Moreover there is obvious sense in statements like "I know more physics than you know French." Or "I am a better runner than you are a
swimmer." Cross-modal comparisons are not impossible, given that we
have some implicit underlying notion of quality. How accurate are such
comparisons? Can we make them at all when the differences between
the individuals are subtle? How do we take into account the difficulty
of the accomplishment? Is being an all-state athlete as distinguished an
accomplishment as being a Merit Scholarship finalist?

How can we understand comparisons like these? Can we adapt
the solutions for small choice to work much further out on the inference limb?

Big Choice

In contrast to small choice, big choice is a situation in which it makes
no sense to insist that all individuals attempt all tasks (e.g., it is of no
interest or value to ask the editor of the school yearbook to quarterback
the football team for a series of plays in order to gauge proficiency in

that context). Making comparisons among individuals after they have made a big choice is quite common. College admissions officers compare students who have chosen to take the French achievement test against those who opted for one in physics, even though their scores are on completely different scales. Companies that reward employees with merit raises usually have a limited pool of money available for raises and, in the quest for an equitable distribution of that pool, must confront such imponderable questions as "Is person A a more worthy carpenter than person B is a salesman?" At the beginning of this chapter I postponed big choice while attempting to deal with the easier problems associated with small choice.

Most of what we have discussed so far leans heavily on sampling responses to choice items from those who hadn't selected them and thus applies primarily to the small-choice situation. Can we make useful comparisons in the context of big choice? Yes, but it depends on the goal of the test. There are many possible goals of a testing program. For now I will consider only three: contest, measurement, and goad to induce change.

When a test is a contest, we are using it to determine a winner. We might wish to choose a subset of examinees for admission, for an award, or for a promotion. In a contest we are principally concerned with fairness. All competitors must be judged under the same rules and conditions. We are not concerned with accuracy, except to require that the test be sufficiently accurate to tell us the order of finish unambiguously.

When a test is used for measurement, we wish to make the most accurate possible determination of some characteristic of an examinee. Usually measurement has associated with it some action; we measure blood pressure and then consider exercise and diet; we measure a child's reading proficiency and then choose suitable books; we measure mathematical proficiency and then choose the next step of instruction. Similarly we employ measurement to determine the efficacy of various interventions. How much did the diet lower blood pressure? How much better was one reading program than another? When measuring we are primarily concerned with accuracy. Anything that reduces error may fairly be included on the test.

When a test is a goad to induce change, we are using the test to influence behavior. Sometimes the test is used as a carrot or a stick to influence the behavior of students; we give the test to get students to study more assiduously. Sometimes the test is used to modify the behavior of teachers; we construct the test to influence teachers' choice of material to be covered. This goal has been characterized as measurement-driven instruction,[15] which has engendered rich and contentious discussions. I will not add to them here.[16] At first blush it might appear that when a test is being used in this way, issues of fairness and measurement precision are not important, although the appearance of fairness may be. However, that is false. When a test is used to induce change, the obvious next question must be, "How well did it work?" If we used the test to get students to study more assiduously, or to study specific material, how much did they do so? How much more have the students learned than they would have under some other condition? The other condition might be "no announced test" or it might be with a test of a different format. There are obvious experimental designs that would allow us to investigate such questions—but all require measurement.[17] Thus, even when the purpose of the test is to influence behavior, that test still ought to satisfy the canons of good measurement practice.

Making useful comparisons in the context of big choice is only possible for tests as contests, at least for the moment. When there is big choice, we can set out rules that will make the contest fair. We are not able to make the inferences that are usually desirable for measurement. Let us begin by considering an instructive (and relatively simple) example, the Ironman Triathlon.

Let us think of the Ironman Triathlon as a three-item test:

1. Swim 2.5 miles. This item takes a great swimmer forty-five minutes.
2. Cycle 125 miles. This item takes a great cyclist more than four hours.

---

[15] Popham 1987.

[16] The interested reader can begin with Gregory Cizek's excellent 1993 paper and work backward through the references provided by him.

[17] It is not uncommon in education for innovations to be tried without an explicit design to aid in determining the efficacy of the intervention. Harold Gulliksen (personal communication, October 1965) was fond of recounting the response he received when he asked what was the control condition against which the particular educational innovation was to be measured. The response was "We didn't have a control because it was *only* an experiment."

3. Run 26.2 miles. This item takes a great runner more than two hours.

Score equals total time. As a contest, it is fair, for everybody knows the scoring rules before they begin.

Suppose we allow choice (pick two of three). Anyone who chooses item 2 is a fool (or doesn't know how to swim).

If we don't tell anyone about the expected amount of time, is the contest with choice still fair? Suppose we assign items to individuals? What would we need to do now to make the test fair?

Possible solution: We could make the items equally difficult. An approximation to such a manipulation is this:

1. Swim 7.5 miles. This item takes a great swimmer more than two hours.
2. Cycle 60 miles. This item takes a great cyclist more than two hours.
3. Run 26.2 miles. This item takes a great runner more than two hours.

Obviously, allowing choice on this modified version (an equilateral triathlon?) is more reasonable than the original formulation, but a lot more work would need to be done to assure that these events are more nearly of equal difficulty than merely using the times of world record holders.

The triathlon is a comparatively new sporting event. The relative dimensions of its component parts may not be what they will eventually become as issues of fairness and competitiveness get worked through with additional data. Thus it is illuminating to examine a more mature event of similar structure; the Olympic decathlon. But before we get to the decathlon let us take a brief theoretical aside to discuss some of the basics of measurement, and what is required to be able to define a winner in an event like the decathlon.

An Aside on Measurement Scales

When we measure anything, the quality of the measurement depends on the instrument we use. More precise measurement requires better tools. We must first decide how much precision is needed for the purpose at hand before we can pick the measuring instrument.

Measurement tools form a continuum that range from primitive to advanced. Let me select four levels of measurement from this range.

At the primitive end we might merely name things: table, chair, horse, dog. Measuring an object means putting it into a category. This sort of measurement is called, for obvious reasons, a *nominal scale*. Such a measurement is not much help for scoring a decathlon, for there is no ordering among the categories. A chair is neither more nor less than a pizza. The sole requirement for a measurement to be considered nominal is that the classification criteria must be unambiguous; an object cannot simultaneously be both a pizza and a chair.

Our next step up the scale is measurement that allows ordering. As such it is called an *ordinal scale*. To be considered ordinal the measure must satisfy the criterion for nominal measurement plus two additional criteria:

1. Connectedness: Either $a \geq b$ or $b \geq a$.
2. Transitivity: If $a \geq b$ and $b \geq c$, then $a \geq c$.

These two criteria seem simple, but a moment's thought reveals how such characteristics separate nominal scale measurement from ordinal. A table is not more than or less than a pizza, hence neither of these two criteria make sense. But if we are to measure some contest we must have a metric in place that allows us to say that either performance a is better than or equal to performance b, or it is worse. Transitivity is also important and its implications are subtle. We will discuss it at greater length shortly. An example of an ordinal scale is Mohs' scale of hardness of minerals, in which any mineral is defined to be harder than another if it can scratch it, and lower if it is scratched. Thus a diamond is very high on the scale, for it will scratch most other things, and talc is very low, for most things will scratch it. Note that this scale satisfies the two requirements. It is easy to see why we must have at least an ordinal scale in order to decide any contest.

Next we come to *interval scales*. Such measurement has to satisfy the requirements of an ordinal scale as well as the additional characteristic that the difference between measurements must be meaningful and have the same meaning throughout the scale. An example is the Celsius scale of temperature. It clearly satisfies the ordinal requirements, but in addition the 10-degree difference between, say, 70 degrees and 60 degrees has the same meaning (in some physical sense) as a 10-degree difference anywhere else on the scale. Interval scale properties are critical for contests whose scores add together pieces from various parts.

Note that ratio inferences, for example, "80 degrees is twice as warm as 40 degrees," make no sense when we have just an interval scale. In order for such inferences to be sensible we need a rational zero. Thus ratio statements of temperature make sense on the Kelvin scale, but not Celsius. This brings us to our last stop on this excursion, the *ratio scale*, which must satisfy all the properties of an interval scale plus have true zero. Thus measurements of length or weight or amount satisfy this requirement; two meters is twice as long as one, ten dollars is twice as much as five, twenty pounds is four times five pounds.

Now we have all the necessary theoretical machinery and vocabulary to move on to our next example.

The Olympic Decathlon

The decathlon is a ten-part track event that is multidimensional. There are strength events like discus, speed events like the 100 meter dash, endurance events like the 1,500 meter run, and events, like the pole vault, that stress agility. Of course underlying all of these events is some notion of generalized athletic ability, which may predict performance in all events reasonably accurately.[18] How is the decathlon scored? In a word, arbitrarily. Each event is counted "equally" in that an equal number of points is allocated for someone who equaled the world record that existed in that event at the time that the scoring rules were specified.[19] How closely one approaches the world record determines the number of points received (i.e., if you are within 90 percent of the

---

[18] Actually it only predicts accurately for top-ranked competitors, who tend to perform "equally" well in all events. There are some athletes who are much better in one event or another, but they tend to have much lower overall performance than generalists who appear more evenly talented.

[19] The Olympic decathlon scoring rules were first established in 1912 and allocated 1,000 points in each event for a world record performance. These scoring rules have been revised in 1936, 1950, 1964, and 1985. It is interesting to note that the 1932 gold medal winner would have finished second under the current (1985) rules.

world record you get 90 percent of the points). As the world records in separate events change, so too does the number of points allocated. If the world record gets 10 percent better, then 10 percent more points are allocated to that event. Let us examine the two relevant questions: Is this accurate measurement? Is this a fair contest?

To judge the accuracy of the procedure as measurement, we need to know the qualities of the scale so defined. Can we consider decathlon scores to be on a ratio scale? Is an athlete who scores 8,000 points twice as good as someone who scores 4,000? Most experts would agree that such statements are nonsensical. Can we consider decathlon scores to be on an interval scale? Is the difference between an athlete who scores 8,000 and one who scores 7,000 in any way the same as the difference between one who scores 2,000 and another who scores 1,000? Again, experts agree that this is not true in any meaningful sense. But, as we shall see, fairness requires that it needs to be approximately true over the (hopefully narrow) regions in the scale where most of the competitors perform.

How successful have the formulators of the scoring scheme for the Olympic Decathlon been in making this contest fair to athletes of all types?

Can we consider decathlon scores to be ordinally scaled? A fair contest must be. It is certainly so within any one event, but across events it is less obvious. This raises an important and interesting issue: If we are using a test as a contest, and we wish that it be fair, we must gather data that would allow us to test the viability of the requirements stated previously. The most interesting condition is that of transitivity. The condition suggests two possible outcomes in a situation involving multidimensional comparisons:

1. There may exist instances in which person A is preferred to person B and person B to person C, and last, person C is preferred to person A. For example, in any NFL season one can almost always construct a number of sequences in which team A beats team B which then beats team C, which later beats team A. This is called an "intransitive triad," and, in football at least, it happens sufficiently often that we cannot always attribute it to random fluctuations. It means that in some multidimensional situations, no ordinal scale exists. This is not necessarily a

bad thing. In this instance it contributes to the health of the professional football betting industry.

2. Data that allow the occurrence of an intransitive triad are not gathered. This means that while the scaling scheme may fail to satisfy the requirements of an ordinal scale, which are crucial for a fair contest, we will never know. This situation occurs in single-elimination tournaments, as well as in big-choice situations.

In a situation involving big choice, we are prevented from knowing if even the connectedness axiom is satisfied. How can we test the viability of this axiom if we can observe only A on one person and only B on another?

To get a better sense of the quality of measurement represented by the decathlon, let us consider what noncontest uses might be made of the scores. The most obvious use would be as a measure of the relative advantage of different training methods. Suppose we had two competing training methods, for example, one emphasizing strength and the other endurance. We then conduct an experiment in which we randomly assign athletes to one or the other of these two methods. In a pretest we get a decathlon score for each competitor and then again after the training period has ended. We then rate each method's efficacy as a function of the mean improvement in total decathlon score. While one might find this an acceptable scheme, it may be less than desirable. Unless all events showed the same direction of effect, some athletes might profit more from a training regime that emphasizes strength, while others might need more endurance. It seems that it would be far better not to combine scores, but rather to treat the ten component scores separately, perhaps as a profile. Of course, each competitor will almost surely want to combine scores to see how much the total has increased, but that is later in the process. The measurement task, in which we are trying to understand the relation between training and performance, is better done at the disaggregated level. It is only for the contest portion that the combination takes place.

We conclude that scoring methods that resemble those used in the decathlon can only be characterized as measurement in an ordinal sense. And thus the measures obtained are only suitable for crude sorts of inferences.

When Is a Contest Fair?

In addition to the requirement of an ordinal scale, fair measurement also requires that all competitors know the rules in advance, that the same rules apply to all competitors equally, and that there is nothing in the rules that gives one competitor an advantage over another because of some characteristic unrelated to the competition. How well do the decathlon rules satisfy these criteria?

Certainly the scoring rules are well known to all competitors, and they apply evenhandedly to everyone. Moreover, the measurements in each event are equally accurate for every competitor. Thus if two competitors throw the shot the same distance, they will get the same number of points. Last, is a competitor placed at a disadvantage because of unrelated characteristics? No; each competitor's score is determined solely by performance in the events. We conclude that the decathlon's scoring rules comprise a fair contest even though they comprise a somewhat limited measuring instrument.

The decathlon represents a good illustration of what can be done with multidimensional tests. Sensible scoring can yield a fair contest, but not good measurement. There has been an attempt to count all events equally, balancing the relative value of an extra inch in the long jump against an extra second in the 1,500 meter run. But no one would contend that they are matched in any formal way. The decathlon is a multidimensional test, but it is not big choice as we have previously defined it. Every competitor provides a score in each event (on every "item"). How much deterioration would result if we add big choice into this mix?

Big choice makes the situation worse. As a real illustration, let us consider a pseudosport that was the subject of a popular 1980s TV program on ABC called *Superstars*. On it athletes from various sports were gathered together to compete in a series of seven different events. Each athlete had to select five events from among the seven. The winner of each event is awarded ten points, second place seven, third place five, and so on. The overall winner was the one who accumulated the most points. Some events were "easier" than others because fewer or lesser athletes elected to compete in that event; nevertheless the same number of points were awarded. This is big choice by our definition, in that there were events in which some athletes could not compete (e.g., Joe Frazier, a former world champion heavyweight boxer, chose not to compete in swimming because he could not swim). Are the scores in such a competition measurement as is commonly defined? No. Is the contest fair? By the rules of fairness described above, perhaps. Although because some of the data were missing (e.g., how well participants would have done on the events they chose not to compete in) the checking of key underlying assumptions is impossible.

If we are careful we can use big choice in a multidimensional context and under limited circumstances to have fair contests. We cannot yet have measurement in this context at a level of accuracy that can be called anything other than crude. Therefore we do not believe that inferences based on such procedures should depend on any characteristic other than their fairness. This being the case, users of big choice should work hard to assure that their scoring schemes are indeed as fair as they can make them.

When Is It Not Fair?

We might term big choice "easy choice," because often big choice is really no choice at all. Consider a "choice" item in which an examinee is asked to discuss the plot of either (*a*) *The Pickwick Papers* or (*b*) *Crime and Punishment* from a Marxist perspective. If the student's teacher chose to include only *The Pickwick Papers* in the syllabus, there really is no choice. At least the student had no choice, because it was not plausible to answer any but a single option. Thus fairness requires the various options to be of equal difficulty. This returns us to the primary point of this account. How are we to ascertain the relative difficulty of big-choice items?

CONCLUSIONS

Can the uncritical use of choice lead us seriously astray? While there are several sources of evidence summarized in this chapter about the size of choice effects, I focused on just one series of exams, the College Board's Advanced Placement tests. Summaries from other sources, albeit analyzed in several different ways, suggest strongly that the Advanced Placement exams are not unusual. In fact they may be considerably better than average.

Experience with allowing choice in an experimental SAT is instructive.[20] It had long been felt by math teachers that it would be better if examinees were allowed to use calculators on the mathematics portion of the SAT. An experiment was performed in which examinees were allowed to use a calculator if they wished. The hope was that it would have no effect on the scores. Alas, calculators improved scores. The experiment also showed that examinees who used more elaborate calculators got higher scores than those who used more rudimentary ones.[21] Sadly, a preliminary announcement had already been made indicating that the future SAT-M would allow examinees the option of using whatever calculator they wished or not using one at all.

A testing situation corresponds to measuring people's heights by having them stand with their backs to a wall. Allowing examinees to bring a calculator to the testing situation, but not knowing for sure whether they had one, nor what kind, corresponds to measuring persons for height while allowing them, unbeknownst to you, to bring a stool of unknown and varying height on which to stand. Accurate and fair measurement is no longer possible.

Our discussion has concentrated on explicitly defined choice in tests, or "alternative questions" in the language of the first half of the twentieth century. However, in the case of portfolio assessment, the element of choice is implicit, and not amenable to many of the kinds of analysis that have been described here. Portfolio assessment, another "bright idea" of some educational theorists, may be more or less structured in its demands on the examinee—that is, it may specify the elements of the portfolio more or less specifically. However, to the extent that the elements of the portfolio are left to the choice of the examinee, portfolio assessment more closely resembles ABC's *Superstars* than even the decathlon. In portfolio assessment, how many forms of the test are created by examinee choice? Often, as many as there are examinees! In this case, such forms cannot be statistically equated. Applicants to universities, or for jobs, present a portfolio of accomplishments. These

[20] Lawrence 1992.
[21] Note that there is no way to know if the more elaborate calculators helped or if more able students chose such calculators. This uncertainty will always be the case when the students make the decision rather than being placed in one category or the other by some controlled process.

portfolios must be compared and evaluated so that the candidates can be ordered with respect to their suitability. Is it possible to do this both fairly and well?

Retreating back to the easier question, is building examinee choice into a test possible? Yes, but it requires extra work. Approaches that ignore the empirical possibility that different items do not have the same difficulty will not satisfy the canons of good testing practice, nor will they yield fair tests. But to assess the difficulty of choice items, one must have responses from a random sample of fully motivated examinees. This requires a special sort of data-gathering effort.

What can we do if the assumptions required for equating are not satisfied across the choice items? If test forms are built that cannot be equated, scores comparing individuals on incomparable forms have their validity compromised by the portion of the test that is not comparable. Thus we cannot fairly allow choice if the process of choosing cannot be adjusted away.

Choice is anathema to standardized testing unless those aspects that characterize the choice are irrelevant to what is being tested. Choice is either impossible or unnecessary.

AFTERWORD

The conclusion I reach in this chapter is bleak. Yet the triage task faced by hiring agents or admission officers is very real. Is there anything that provides even a ray of hope? I think so. Specifically,

1. If there are some common elements associated with all applicants (e.g., they all take the same exam), a fair ordering of the applicants can begin with the ordering on that exam.
2. If there are vast differences between candidates on items with choice (e.g., one candidate won an Olympic swimming medal while still in high school whereas her competitor won fourth place in the school's French competition) fair conclusions can be drawn about relative commitment, accomplishment, and proficiency. Mozart was a better musician than I am a swimmer. But the smaller the differences, the less valuable the evidence is for making comparative judgments.

3. Sometimes other issues enter into the decision. Remember the problem that Samantha Stewart, the admissions director, faced at the very beginning of this chapter. Although there was no way for her to be able to tell whether one candidate was a better violinist than the other was a quarterback, the decision was, in the end, easy. The university had desperate need of a quarterback but had plenty of violinists. This solution illustrates an old and honored strategy, usually known as the principle of "It don't make no nevermind." When faced with a difficult problem you can't solve, find a way to avoid it.

I hope that I have made the case for avoiding, as much as is possible, giving choice. There are enough instances where there is no alternative but to have choice; we should not add to them. Last let me reiterate a point I made earlier—when choice is added, more able subgroups of examinees will choose more wisely than less able subgroups. This has been shown to exacerbate the differences between groups, hardly the outcome hoped for by proponents of providing choice toward the goal of fairer testing.

7

❧ ❧

What If Choice Is Part of the Test?

*But choose wisely, for while the true Grail will bring
you life, the false Grail will take it from you.*
—Grail Knight in *Indiana Jones and the Last Crusade*

In their search for the Holy Grail, both Walter Donovan and Indiana
Jones arrived at the Canyon of the Crescent Moon with great anticipation.
But after all of the other challenges had been met, the last test involved
choice. The unfortunate Mr. Donovan chose first, and in the words of the
Grail Knight, "He chose poorly." The consequences were severe.

In modern society we too must pass many tests, and we too must
learn to choose wisely. The consequences are sometimes serious,
although hopefully not as profound as for poor Walter Donovan.

In the last chapter we discussed the issues surrounding implementing choice in any fair assessment. I fear that the message I left you
with was not sanguine. Allowing an examinee to choose which items
to answer on a standardized test seems like a humane way to allow
people to showcase their talents most fully. But alas, we saw that too
often people do not choose wisely. In fact, those of lesser ability tend to
choose less wisely than those who perform better. Thus allowing choice
tends to exacerbate group differences.

Is this all there is? Some defenders of choice have come out with
another compelling argument, which is sufficiently reasonable that I
have chosen to include this small chapter just for its consideration.

The alternative to trying to make all examinee-selected choices
within a choice question of equal difficulty is to consider the entire set

of questions with choices as a single item.[1] Thus the choice is part of the item. If you make a poor choice and select an especially difficult option to respond to, that is considered in exactly the same way as if you wrote a poor answer.

Under what circumstances is this a plausible and fair approach? And, to the point of this chapter, what consequences result from this point of view?

It seems to me that two issues arise immediately:

1. If we want to include the choice as part of the item, we must believe that choosing wisely uses the same knowledge and skills that are required for answering the question. If not, what are we testing?

As a counterexample, suppose we asked examinees in an English literature exam to write an essay on one of two topics. Each topic was written on a piece of paper. One was under a steel dome that weighed 160 pounds, and was quite easy. The other was under an aluminum dome weighing just 5 pounds, but was relatively difficult. It was found that physically stronger examinees (most of whom were men) lifted both domes and then opted for the easier topic. Physically weaker examinees (most of whom were women) couldn't budge the heavy dome and were forced to answer the more difficult question. Since knowledge of English literature has nothing to do with physical strength, making the "choice" part of the question is neither appropriate nor fair.

2. We must believe that the choice is being made by the examinees and not by their teachers. Course curricula are fluid and the choice of which topics the instructor decides to include and which to omit is sometimes arbitrary. If the choice options are of unequal difficulty, and the easier option was not covered in a student's course, having examinee choice disadvantages those who, through no fault of their own, had to answer the more difficult question.

Let us assume for the moment that through dint of mighty effort an exam is prepared in which the choice items are carefully constructed

---

[1] Using the currently correct jargon this "super item" should, properly, be called a testlet.

so that the skills related to choosing wisely are well established and agreed by all participants to be a legitimate part of the curriculum that is being tested and that all options available could, plausibly, be asked of each examinee.

If this is all true, it leads to a remarkable and surprising result—we can offer choice on an essay test and obtain satisfactory results without grading the essays! In fact, the examinees don't even have to write the essays; it is enough that they merely indicate their preferences.

EVIDENCE: THE 1989 ADVANCED PLACEMENT EXAMINATION IN CHEMISTRY

The evidence for this illustration is from the five constructed response items in Part II, Section D of the 1989 Advanced Placement Examination in Chemistry.[2] Section D has five items of which the examinee must answer just three.[3]

This form of the exam was taken by approximately 18,000 students in 1989.[4] These items are problems that are scored on a scale from 0 to 8 using a rigorous analytic scoring scheme.

Since examinees must answer three out of the five items, a total of ten choice groups were formed, with each group taking a somewhat different test than the others. Because each group had at least one problem in common with every other group, we are able to use this overlap to place all examinee-selected forms onto a common scale.[5] The results are summarized in table 7.1.

The score scale used had an average of 500; thus those examinees who chose the first three items (1, 2, and 3) scored considerably lower than any other group. Next, the groups labeled 2 through 7 were

[2] A full description of this test, the examinee population, and the scoring model is found in Wainer, Wang, and Thissen 1994.

[3] This section accounts for 19 percent of the total grade.

[4] The test form has been released and interested readers may obtain copies of it with the answers and a full description of the scoring methodology from the College Board.

[5] We did this by fitting a polytomous IRT model to all ten forms simultaneously (see Wainer, Wang, and Thissen 1994 for details). As part of this fitting procedure we obtained estimates of the mean value of each choice group's proficiency as well as the marginal reliability of this section of the test.

TABLE 7.1
Scores of Examinees as a Function of the Problems They Chose

Group	Problems chosen	Mean group score	Sample size
1	1, 2, 3	398	2,555
2	2, 3, 5	496	121
3	1, 2, 4	500	5,227
4	1, 3, 5	504	753
5	1, 3, 4	508	4,918
6	2, 3, 4	508	1,392
7	1, 2, 5	509	457
8	2, 4, 5	540	407
9	3, 4, 5	543	98
10	1, 4, 5	547	1,707

essentially indistinguishable in performance from one another. Last, groups 8, 9, and 10 were the best-performing groups. The average reliability of the ten overlapping forms of this three-item test was a shade less than 0.60.[6]

Suppose we think of Section D as a single "item" with an examinee falling into one of ten possible categories, and the estimated score of each examinee is the mean score of everyone in his or her category. How reliable is this one-item test?[7] After doing the appropriate calculation we discover that the reliability of this "choice item" is .15. While .15 is less than .60, it is also larger than zero, and it is easier to obtain.

Consider a "choice test" built of "items" like Section D, except that instead of asking examinees to pick three of the five questions and answer them, we ask them to indicate which three questions they

---

[6] *Reliability* is a number between 0 and 1 that characterizes the stability of the score. A reliability of 0 means that the score is essentially just a random number, having nothing whatever to do with your proficiency. A reliability of 1 means that the score is errorless. Most professionally built standardized tests have reliability around .9. The reliability of .6 on this small section of a test is well within professional standards.

[7] We can calculate an analog of reliability, the squared correlation of proficiency (θ) with estimated proficiency ($\hat{\theta}$) from the between group variance [$\mathrm{var}(\mu_i)$] and the within-group variance (which is here fixed at 100). This index of reliability,

$$\{r^2(\hat{\theta}, \theta) = \mathrm{var}(\mu_i) \,/\, [\mathrm{var}(\mu_i) + 100]\},$$

is easily calculated.

TABLE 7.2
Guide for Building a Choice Test of Specified Reliability

Test length[a]	Reliability
2	.1
5	.2
8	.3
12	.4
19	.5
28	.6
44	.7
75	.8
168	.9

[a] Measured in number of binary choices.

would answer, and then go on to the next "item." This takes less time for the examinee and is far easier to score.

Of course with a reliability of only .15, this is not much of a test. But suppose we had two such items, each with a reliability of .15. This new test would have a reliability of .26. And, to get to the end of the story, if we had eight such "items" it would have a reliability of .6, the same as the current form.

Thus, if we truly believe that the act of choosing is accessing the same key skills and knowledge as the specific questions asked, we have found a way to measure those skills with far less effort (for both the examinee and the test scorer) than would have been required if the examinee actually had to answer the questions.

Such a test need not be made of units in which the examinee must choose three of five. It could be binary, in which the examinee is presented with a pair of items and must choose one of them. In such a situation, if the items were constructed to be like the AP Chemistry test, the number of such binary choices needed for any prespecified reliability is shown in table 7.2.

Of course all of these calculations are predicated on having items to be chosen from that have the properties of those comprising Section D for the 1989 AP Chemistry examination: The items must vary substantially in difficulty, and this must be more or less apparent to the examinees, depending on their proficiency.

CONCLUSION AND DISCUSSION

How much information is obtained by requiring examinees to actually answer questions, and then grading them? This effort has some reward for the AP Chemistry test, where the constructed response section is analytically scored. But how much are these rewards diminished when the test's scoring scheme is less rigorous?

Table 7.3 shows the reliabilities for the constructed response sections of all Advanced Placement tests. Note that there is very little overlap between the distributions of reliability for analytically and holistically scored tests,[8] the latter being considerably less reliable. Holistic, in this context, means that the scorer, after reading the examinee's response, assesses its value as a whole, rather than by measuring different aspects separately and adding them up in some fashion. Chemistry is a little better than average among analytically scored tests with a reliability of .78 for its constructed response sections.

It is sobering to consider how a test that uses only the options chosen would compare to a less reliable test (i.e., any of the holistically scored tests). The structure of such a choice test might be to offer a set of, say, ten candidate essay topics, and ask the examinees to choose four topics that they would like to write on. And then stop.

It is not my intention to suggest that it is better to have examinees choose questions to answer than it is to actually have them answer them. I observe only that if the purpose is measurement, a great deal of information can be obtained from the choices made. Moreover, one should feel cautioned if the test administration and scoring schema that one is using yields a measuring instrument of only about the same accuracy that would have been obtained ignoring the performance of the examinee entirely.

This is what I like best about science. With only a small investment in fact, we can garner huge dividends in conjecture.

---

[8] The term *holistic* is likely derived from (after Thompson 1917) "what the Greeks called 'αρμονία. This is something exhibited not only by a lyre in tune, but by all the handiwork of craftsmen, and by all that is "put together" by art or nature. It is the "compositeness of any composite whole"; and, like the cognate terms κρσις or σύνθεσις, implies a balance or attunement."

TABLE 7.3
Reliabilities of the Constructed Response Sections of AP Tests

Analytically scored	Score reliability	Holistically scored
Calculus AB	.85	
Physics B	.84	
Computer Science	.82	
Calculus BC	.80	
French Language	.79	
Chemistry	.78	
Latin-Virgil	.77	
Latin–Catullus-Horace	.76	
Physics C–Electricity	.74	
Music Theory, Biology	.73	
Spanish Language	.72	
Physics C–Mechanics	.70	History of Art
	.69	French Literature
	.63	Spanish Literature
	.60	English Language & Composition
	.56	English Literature & Composition
German Language	.50	
	.49	American History
	.48	European History
	.29	Music: Listening & Literature

8

~~ ~~

A Little Ignorance Is a Dangerous Thing

How Statistics Rescued a Damsel in Distress

A little ignorance is a dangerous thing.
—apologies to Alexander Pope

Since the passage of the No Child Left Behind Act the role of standard-ized test scores in contemporary education has grown. Students have been tested, and teachers, schools, districts, and states have been judged by the outcome. The pressure to get high scores has increased, and con-cern about cheating has increased apace. School officials desperately want high scores, but simultaneously do not want even the appear-ance of any malfeasance. Thus, after sixteen of the twenty-five students in Jenny Jones's third-grade class at the Squire Allworthy Elementary School obtained perfect scores on the state's math test, it was not entirely a surprise that a preliminary investigation took place. The concern of the principal arose because only about 2 percent of all third-graders in the state had perfect scores, and so this result, as welcome as it was, seemed so unlikely that it was bound to attract unwanted attention.

The investigation began with a discussion between the principal and Ms Jones, in which Ms. Jones explained that she followed all of the rules specified by Ms. Blifil, a teacher designated by the principal as the admin-istrator of the exam. One of the rules that Ms. Blifil sent to teachers giving the exam was "point and look": The proctor of the exam was instructed to stroll around the class during the administration of the exam, and if

This chapter developed from P. Baldwin and H. Wainer, "A Little Ignorance: How Statistics Rescued a Damsel in Distress," *Chance*, 22(3) (2009): 51–55.

she saw a student doing something incorrectly, she should point to that item and look at the student. Ms. Jones did not proctor the exam, for she was occupied with administering it individually to a student in special education, but she instructed an aide on how to serve as proctor.

"Point and look" seemed to be forbidden by the state's rules for test administration, for page 11 of the administrators' manual says,

> Be sure students understand the directions and how to mark answers. Assist them with test-taking mechanics, but be careful not to inadvertently give hints or clues that indicate the answer or help eliminate answer choices.

That pretty much disqualifies "point and look."

The school's investigation found what they believed to be the cause of the high scores earned by Ms. Jones's class. To cement this conclusion the school administration brought in an expert, a Dr. Thwackum, to confirm that indeed the obtained test results were too good to be true. Dr. Thwackum was a young PhD who had studied measurement in graduate school. He was asked if the results obtained on the math exam were sufficiently unlikely to justify concluding that students had been inappropriately aided by the exam proctor. Dr. Thwackum billed the district for ninety minutes of his time and concluded that indeed such a result was so unlikely that it was not plausible that the test had been administered fairly.

Ms. Jones was disciplined, suspended without pay for a month, and given an "unsatisfactory" rating. Her pay increment for the year was eliminated, and her service for the year did not count toward her seniority. Through her union she filed an appeal.

The union hired statisticians to look into the matter more carefully. This chapter is a description of what the statisticians found.

NO HARM, NO FOUL; OR, THE BURDEN OF PROOF LIES UPON HIM WHO AFFIRMS, NOT UPON HIM WHO DENIES[1]

"No harm, no foul" and the presumption of innocence help constitute the foundations upon which the great institutions of basketball and

---

[1] *Ei incumbit probatio qui dicit, non qui negat.*

justice, respectively, rest. The adjudication of Ms. Jones's appeal relied heavily on both principles. Ms. Jones admitted to instructing the exam proctor about the "point and look" rule—her culpability on this point is not in dispute. However, she was *not* disciplined for incorrectly instructing the proctor; rather she was disciplined for the alleged *effect* of the proctor's behavior. This distinction places a much greater burden on the school because it must show that the "point and look" intervention not only took place but that it had an effect. That is, the school must demonstrate that Ms. Jones's rule violation (foul) unfairly improved her students' scores (harm). Failure to show such an effect exculpates her.

Further, here the burden of proof lies on the accuser, not the accused. That is, Ms. Jones is presumed innocent unless the school can prove otherwise. Moreover, the scarcity of high-quality, student-level data made proving that the effect of "point and look" could not be zero much more challenging than proving that it could have been.

The subsequent investigation had two parts. The first was to show that it is believable that the cause (the "point and look" rule) had no effect, and the second and larger part was to estimate the size of the alleged effect (the improvement in performance attributable to this cause) or—as we shall discuss—show that the size of the effect could have been zero.

The Cause

Because the principle of "No harm, no foul" makes the effect—not the cause—of primary concern, our interest in the cause is limited to showing that it is plausible that the aide's behavior had no effect on children's scores. This is not difficult to imagine if it is recalled that Ms. Jones's third-grade class was populated with eight-year-olds. Getting them to sit still and concentrate on a lengthy exam is roughly akin to herding parakeets. In addition there were more than ten forms of the test that were handed out at random to the class so that the aide, in looking down on any specific exam at random was unlikely to be seeing the same question that she saw previously. So what was the kind of event that is likely to have led to her "pointing and looking"? She might have pointed to a question that had been inadvertently omitted, or perhaps suggested that a student should take the pencil out of his nose or stop hitting the student just in front of him.

The developers of the test surely had such activities in mind when they wrote the test manual, for on page 8 of the instructions they said,

> Remind students who finish early to check their work in that section of the test for completeness and accuracy and to attempt to answer every question.

So indeed it is quite plausible that the aide's activities were benign and had little or no effect on test scores. Given this possibility, both the prosecution and the defendants sought to measure the alleged effect: Dr. Thwackum seeking to show that the effect could not have been zero, while the statisticians tried to show that the effect *could* have been zero. Of course, this was an observational study, not an experiment. We don't know the counterfactual result of how the children would have done had the aide behaved differently. And so the analysis must use external information, untestable assumptions, and the other tools of observational studies.

The Effect

First, we must try to understand how Dr. Thwackum so quickly arrived at his decisive conclusion. Had he been more naive, he might have computed the probability of sixteen out of twenty-five perfect scores based on the statewide result of 2 percent perfect scores. But he knew that that would have assumed that all students were equally likely to get a perfect score. He must have known that this was an incorrect assumption and that he needed to condition on some information that would allow him to distinguish among students. It is well established that all valid tests of mental ability are related to one another. For example, the verbal and mathematical portions of the SAT correlate 0.7 with each other; about the same as the correlation between the heights of parents and children.

Happily, Dr. Thwackum had, close at hand, the results of a reading test used by the state (with the unlikely name of DIBELS) for the students who were in Ms. Jones's class. He built a model using the DIBELS score to predict the math score from an independent sample and found, using this model with the DIBELS scores as the independent variable, that it predicted not a single perfect score on the math test for any of the students in Ms. Jones's class. As far as Dr. Thwackum was concerned that sealed the case against the unfortunate Ms. Jones.

But, it turned out that, aside from being immediately available, DIBELS has little going for it. It is a very short and narrowly focused test that uses one-minute reading passages scored in a rudimentary fashion. It can be reliably scored but it has little generality of inference. An influential study of its validity concluded that "DIBELS mis-predicts reading performance on other assessments much of the time, and at best is a measure of who reads quickly without regard to whether the reader comprehends what is read."[2] And, more to the point of this investigation, when Dr. Thwackum used DIBELS to predict math scores, the correlation between the two was approximately 0.4. Thus it wasn't surprising that the predicted math scores were shrunken toward the overall average score and no perfect scores were portended.

Is there a more informative way to study this? First we must reconcile ourselves to the reality that additional data are limited. What were available were the reading and math scaled scores for all the students in the school district containing Squire Allworthy School and some state- and countywide summary data. Failure to accommodate the limitations of these data may produce a desirable result but not one that bears scrutiny (as Dr. Thwackum discovered). We can begin by noting that the third-grade math test has no top; hence it discriminates badly at the high end. This is akin to measuring height with a ruler that only extends to six feet. It works perfectly well for a large portion of the population, but it groups together all individuals whose heights exceed its upper limit.

This result is obvious in the frequency distribution of raw scores in figure 8.1. Had the test been constructed to discriminate among more proficient students, the right side of the distribution would resemble the left side, yielding the familiar symmetric bell-shaped curve.

Although only 2 percent of all third-graders statewide had perfect scores of 61 on the test, about 22 percent had scores 58 or greater. There is only a very small difference in performance between perfect and very good. In fact, more than half the children (54 percent) taking this test scored 53 or greater. Thus the test does not distinguish very well among

---

[2] Pressley, Hilden, and Shankland 2002.

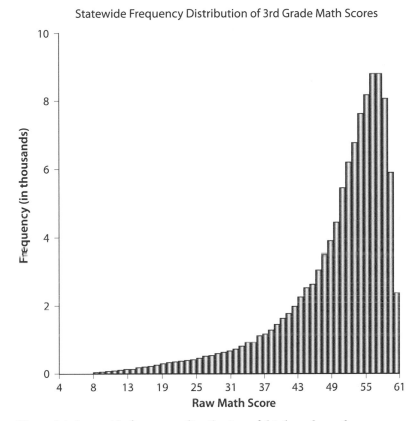

Figure 8.1. Statewide frequency distribution of third-grade math scores

the best students—few would conclude that a third-grader who gets 58 right out of 61 on a math test is demonstrably worse than one who got 61 right. And no one knowledgeable about the psychometric variability of tests would claim that such a score difference was reliable enough to replicate in repeated testing.

But figure 8.1 is for the entire state. What about this particular county? What about Squire Allworthy Elementary School? To answer this we can compare the county-level, school-level, and classroom-level results with the state using the summary data available to us. One such summary for reading—which is not in dispute—is shown in table 8.1.

From this we see that the county does much better than the state as a whole, the district does better than the county, Squire Allworthy

TABLE 8.1
Third-Grade Reading 2006: Performance Levels

	Advanced	Proficient	Basic	Below basic
State	31%	38%	15%	16%
County	45%	36%	10%	9%
District	55%	35%	6%	4%
Squire Allworthy School	58%	35%	6%	1%
Ms. Jones's students	84%	16%	0%	0%

does better still with fully 93 percent of its students being classified as Advanced or Proficient, and Ms. Jones's students perform best, with *all* examinees scoring at the Proficient or Advanced level in reading. Clearly, Ms. Jones's students are in elite company, performing at a very high level compared to other third-graders in the state. Let us add that within district, reading and math scores correlated positively and reasonably strongly.

If we build a model using reading to predict math, we find the regression effect makes it impossible to predict a perfect math score—even from a perfect reading score. In part, this is due to the ceiling effect we discussed previously (the prediction model fails to account for the artificially homogeneous scores at the upper end of the scale) and in part it's due to the modest relationship between reading and math scores. Thus, when Dr. Thwackum used this approach, with an even poorer predictor, DIBELS scores, it came as no surprise that Ms. Jones's students' performance seemed implausible.

Observations

Dr. Thwackum's strategy was not suitable for these data because it must, perforce underpredict high performers. An even simpler approach, which circumvents this problem, is to look only at examinees with perfect math scores. In addition to Ms. Jones's sixteen students with perfect scores, there were twenty-three non-Jones students with perfect math scores within the Squire Allworthy School's district. We can compare reading scores for Ms. Jones's students with those for non-Jones students. There are three possible outcomes here: (1) Ms. Jones's students do better than non-Jones students, (2) all students perform the same, or (3) Ms. Jones's students do worse than non-Jones students. We observed above that there was a modestly strong positive relationship between reading and math proficiency. For this subset of perfect math performers, there is no variability among scores, so no relationship between reading and math can be observed. Nevertheless, failure to observe any relationship can be plausibly attributed to the ceiling effect discussed above rather than a true absence of relationship between reading and math proficiency. So we could reasonably suggest that if Ms. Jones's perfect performers were unfairly aided, their reading scores should be lower on average than non-Jones perfect performers. That is, if option (3) (Ms. Jones's students do worse than non-Jones students) is shown to be true, it could be used as evidence in support of the school district's case against Ms. Jones. However, if Ms. Jones's students do as well or better than non-Jones students—options (1) and (2) above—or if we lack the power to identify any differences, we must conclude that the effect *could* have been zero, at least based on this analysis.

Typically, if we wanted to compare reading score means for Ms. Jones's sixteen students and the districts' twenty-three students with perfect math scores, we would make some distributional assumptions and perform a statistical test. However, even that is not necessary here because Ms. Jones's students' reading mean is *higher* than the districts' students' mean. The districts' twenty-three students with perfect math scores had a mean reading score of 1549, whereas the sixteen students in Ms. Jones's class with perfect math scores had a mean reading score of 1650.[3]

The box plots in figure 8.2 compare the distribution of reading scores for two groups of students with perfect math scores. This plot follows common convention, with the box containing the middle 50 percent of the data and the cross line representing the median. The dotted vertical lines depict the upper and lower quarters of the data. The two small circles represent two unusual points.

We can see that Ms. Jones's students' reading scores are not below the reference group's (as would be expected had her intervention produced

---

[3] For those assiduous and technically skilled readers who wish to do their own statistical test, the standard errors were 30 and 41 for the district's students and Ms. Jones's students respectively.

Reading Scores for Students with Perfect Math Scores

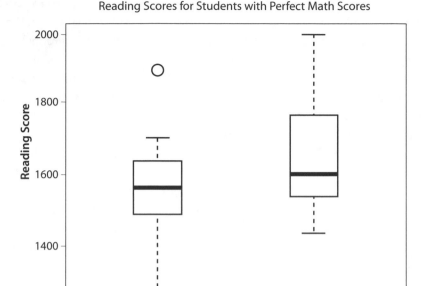

Figure 8.2. Reading scores for students with perfect math scores

the alleged effect). On the contrary: her sixteen perfect math students did noticeably better on reading than non-Jones students who earned perfect math scores. This suggests that Ms. Jones's students' perfect math scores are not inconsistent with their reading scores. And, in fact, if the math test had a higher top, her students would be expected to do better still.

Thus based on the data we have available we cannot reject the hypothesis that Ms. Jones's students came by their scores honestly, for there is no empirical evidence that Ms. Jones's intervention produced an effect of any kind: her students' scores appear no less legitimate than those of students from other classes in the district.

The Outcome

On December 5, 2008, there was an arbitration hearing to decide the outcome of Ms. Jones's appeal. Faced with these results the representatives of the district decided to settle a few minutes in advance of the hearing. Ms. Jones's pay and seniority were restored and her "unsatisfactory" rating was replaced with one better suited to an exemplary teacher whose students perform at the highest levels.

Ms. Blifil was relieved of further responsibility in the oversight of standardized exams and the practice of "point and look" was retired.

The statisticians who did these analyses were rewarded with Ms. Jones's gratitude, the knowledge that they helped rectify a grievous wrong, and a modest honorarium.

Hopefully, Dr. Thwackum learned that a little ignorance is a dangerous thing.

9

⌘ ⌘

Assessing Teachers from Student Scores

On the Practicality of Value-Added Models

Nobody ever got into trouble docking too slowly.
—Anonymous sailor

The less you know, the more you believe.
—Bono

In chapter 8 we saw how administrators of a school district, unused to the rigorous use of evidence in decision making, made a serious error in assessing the performance of one teacher. In this chapter we examine how the uncritical use of complex statistical machinery holds the promise of extending these sorts of errors nationwide.

The No Child Left Behind Act (NCLB) has focused attention on having highly qualified teachers in every classroom. The determination of "highly qualified" is based on such criteria as academic training, experience, and state licensure requirements. But there has been increased pressure to move beyond traditional requirements in our efforts to identify competent teachers. Indeed, if we can reliably identify those individuals who are exemplary, as well as those who are especially in need of support, we will have taken an important step forward.

This chapter developed from H. Braun and H. Wainer, "Value-Added Assessment," in *Handbook of Statistics*, vol. 27, *Psychometrics*, ed. C. R. Rao and S. Sinharay (Amsterdam: Elsevier Science, 2007), 867–892.

Accountability in NCLB has a strong empirical component: Schools are judged on the basis of whether increasingly large proportions of their students achieve their state's proficiency standard. It is natural to ask if there is an empirical basis for evaluating teachers. Indeed, if good teaching is critical to student learning, then can't student learning (or its absence) tell us something about the quality of teaching? While the logic seems unassailable, it is far from straightforward to devise a practical system that embodies this reasoning. Over the last decade or so a number of solutions have been proposed and put to work. They are usually referred to by the generic term *value-added models* and abbreviated as VAM.

Value-added models rely on complex statistical machinery, not easily explained. Ironically there is a marked contrast between the enthusiasm of those who accept the claims of VAM developers and would like to use it, and reservations expressed by those who have studied its technical merits. It appears, at least at the moment, that the more you know about VAM the less faith you have in the validity of inferences drawn from it.

This chapter has four parts. In the next section I provide a nontechnical description of VAM, and in the following three sections I discuss the three principal challenges facing its viable implementation: causal inference, missing data, and the stringency of the requirements placed on the test instruments themselves.

SOME HOWS AND WHYS OF VAM

The principal claim made by the developers of VAM is that through the analysis of changes in student test scores from one year to the next they can objectively isolate the contributions of teachers and schools to student learning.[1] If this claim proves to be true, VAM could become a powerful tool for both teachers' professional development and teachers' evaluation.

This approach represents an important divergence from the path specified by the "adequate yearly progress" provisions of the NCLB Act, for it focuses on the gain each student makes rather than the proportion of students who attain some particular standard. VAM's attention to

---

[1] Sanders, Saxton, and Horn 1997.

individual student's longitudinal data to measure their progress seems filled with common sense and fairness.

There are many models that fall under the general heading of VAM. One of the most widely used was developed and programmed by William Sanders and his colleagues.[2] It was developed for use in Tennessee and has been in place there for more than a decade under the name Tennessee Value-Added Assessment System. It has also been called the "layered model" because of the way that each of its annual component pieces is layered on top of one another.

The model itself begins simply by representing a student's test score in the first year, y_1, as the sum of the district's average for that grade, subject and year, say μ_1, and the incremental contribution of the teacher, say θ_1, and systematic and unsystematic errors, say ε_1. When these pieces are put together we obtain a simple equation for the first year,

$$y_1 = \mu_1 + \theta_1 + \varepsilon_1,\tag{9.1}$$

or

Student's score (1) = district average (1) + teacher effect (1) + error (1).

There are similar equations for the second, third, fourth, and fifth years, and it is instructive to look at the second year's equation, which looks like the first year's except it contains a term for the teacher's effect from the previous year,

$$y_2 = \mu_2 + \theta_1 + \theta_2 + \varepsilon_2,\tag{9.2}$$

or

Student's score (2) = district average (2) + teacher effect (1)
+ teacher (2) + error (2).

To assess the value added $(y_2 - y_1)$ we merely subtract equation (9.1) from equation (9.2) and note that the effect of the teacher from the first year has conveniently dropped out. While this is statistically convenient, because it leaves us with fewer parameters to estimate, does it make sense? Some have argued that although a teacher's effect lingers on beyond the year that the student had her or him, that effect is likely to shrink with time. Although such a model is less convenient

---

[2] Ballou, Sanders, and Wright 2004.

to estimate, in the opinion of many it more realistically mirrors reality. But, not surprisingly, the estimate of the size of a teacher's effect varies depending upon the choice of the model. How large this "choice of model" effect is, relative to the size of the "teacher effect"[3] is yet to be determined. Obviously if it is large it diminishes the practicality of the methodology. Some recent research from the Rand Corporation[4] shows that a shift from the layered model to one that estimates the size of the change of a teacher's effect from one year to the next suggests that almost half of the teacher effect is accounted for by the choice of model.

An issue of critical importance that I shall return to in the section below titled "Do Tests Provide the Evidence for the Inferences VAM Would Have Us Make?" pertains to the estimation of student effects. Obviously one cannot partition student effect from teacher effect without some information on how the same students perform with other teachers. In practice, using longitudinal data and obtaining measures of student performance in other years can resolve this issue. The decade of Tennessee's experience with VAM has led to a requirement of at least three years' data. This requirement raises the obvious concerns when (1) some data are missing (see below, the section titled "Dealing with Missing or Erroneous Data: The Second Challenge") and (2) the meaning of what is being tested changes as time goes on (see below, the section titled "Do Tests Provide the Evidence for the Inferences VAM Would Have Us Make?").

DRAWING CAUSAL INFERENCES: THE FIRST CHALLENGE

The goal of VAM is causal inference.[5] When we observe that the "effect" of being in Mr. Jones's class is a gain of twelve points, we would like

---

[3] The important model parameter "teacher effect" is misnamed. It represents the variability associated with the classroom, whose value is surely affected by the teacher as well as the extent of crowdedness of the room, the comfort of its furniture and temperature, as well as the makeup of the student body. A fourth-grader with frequent difficulty in bladder control will be disruptive of learning and not under the control of the teacher. A better term would be "classroom effect."

[4] McCaffrey, personal communication, October 13, 2004.

[5] The introduction of this section borrows heavily from a 2005 essay written by Paul Holland entitled "Counterfactuals" that he prepared for the *Encyclopedia of Statistics in Behavioral Science*

to interpret "effect" as "effectiveness." But compared to what? Surely we know enough not to attribute a gain of four inches in height to having been in Mr. Jones's class, why should we attribute a gain of twelve points in mathematics performance to Mr. Jones? The implication is that had the student been in a different class the gain would have been different, and the effectiveness of Mr. Jones is related to the difference between the gain shown in his class and the unobserved gain that would have occurred had the child been in a different class.

This idea of estimating a causal effect by looking at the difference between what happened and what we think would have happened is what makes causal inference so difficult. It always involves a counterfactual conditional. The term *counterfactual conditional* is used in logical analysis to refer to any expression of the general form "If A were the case. then B would be the case," and in order to be counterfactual or contrary to fact, A must be false or untrue in the world.

There are many examples:

1. If kangaroos had no tails, they would topple over.
2. If an hour ago I had taken two aspirins instead of just a glass of water, my headache would now be gone.

Perhaps the most obnoxious counterfactuals in any language are those of the form:

3. If I were you, I would . . .

Let us explore more deeply the connection between counterfactual conditionals and references to causation. A good place to start is with the language used by Hume in his famous discussion of causation, where he embedded two definitions:

> We may define a cause to be an object followed by another, and where all the objects, similar to the first, are followed by objects similar to the second. Or, in other words, where, if the first object had not been, the second would never had existed.

Compare the factual first definition where one object *is* followed by another and the counterfactual second definition where, counterfactually, it is supposed that if the first object "had not been," then the second object would not have been either.

It is the connection between counterfactuals and causation that makes them relevant to behavioral science research. It is difficult, if not impossible, to give causal interpretations to the results of statistical calculations without using counterfactual language. The term *counterfactual* is often used as a synonym for control group or comparison. What is the counterfactual? This usage usually just means, "To what is the treatment being compared?" It is a sensible question because the effect of a treatment is always relative to some other treatment. In educational research this simple observation can be quite important, and "What is the counterfactual?" is always worth asking and answering.

Let us return to student testing. Suppose that we find that a student's test performance improves from a score of X to a score of Y after some educational intervention. We might then be tempted to attribute the pretest–posttest change, Y – X, to the intervening educational experience—that is, to use the gain score as a measure of the improvement due to the intervention. However, this is behavioral science and not the tightly controlled "before-after" measurements made in a physics laboratory. There are many other possible explanations of the gain, Y – X. Some of the more obvious are the following:

1. Simple maturation (he was forty-eight inches tall at the beginning of the school year and fifty-one inches tall at the end)
2. Other educational experiences occurring during the relevant time period
3. Differences in either the tests or the testing conditions at pre- and posttest.

From Hume we see that what is important is what the value of Y *would have been* if the student *had not* had the educational experiences that the intervention entailed.

Call this score value Y*. Thus enter counterfactuals. Y* is not directly observed for the student; that is, he or she *did have* the educational intervention of interest, so asking for what his or her posttest score *would have been* had he or she *not had it* is asking for information collected under conditions that are contrary to fact. Hence, it is not the difference Y – X that is of causal interest, but the difference Y – Y*, and the gain score has a causal significance only if X can serve as a substitute for the counterfactual Y*.

In physical-science laboratory experiments this *counterfactual substitution* is often easy to make (for example, if we had not heated the bar, its length would have remained the same), but it is rarely believable in most behavioral science applications of any consequence.

In fact, justifying the substitution of data observed on a control or comparison group for what the outcomes would have been in the treatment group had they not had the treatment, that is, justifying the counterfactual substitution, is the key issue in all of causal inference.

What are the kinds of inferences that users of VAM are likely to want to make? A change score like "The students in Mr. Jones's class gained an average of twelve points" is a fine descriptive statement. They did indeed gain twelve points on average. And, with a little work, and some assumptions, one could also fashion a confidence bound around that gain to characterize its stochastic variability. But it is a slippery slope from description to causality, and it is easy to see how the users of such a result could begin to infer that the children gained twelve points "because" they had Mr. Jones. To be able to draw this inference, we would need to know what gain the students would have made had they had a different teacher. This is the counterfactual.

We can begin to understand this counterfactual by asking what are the alternatives to Mr. Jones. Let us suppose that there was another teacher, Ms. Smith, whose class gained twenty points on average. Can we legitimately infer that the students in Mr. Jones's class would've gained eight additional points if they had only been so fortunate to be taught by Ms. Smith? What would allow us to make this inference? If Mr. Jones class was made up of students with a history of diminished performance and Ms. Smith's class was part of the gifted and talented program, would we draw the same conclusion? In fact it is only if we can reasonably believe that both classes were identical, on average, is such an inference plausible. If the classes were filled by selecting students at random for one or the other class, this assumption of homogeneity begins to be reasonable. How often are classes made up at random? Even if such student allocation is attempted, in practice the randomization is often compromised by scheduling difficulties, parental requests, team practices, and the like.[6]

---

[6] Random assignment, the usual panacea for problems with diverse populations, does not handle all issues here. Suppose there is a single, very disruptive student. That student is likely to adversely affect the teacher's efficacy. Even if all teachers were equally likely

Can we adjust statistically for differences in classroom composition caused by shortcomings in the allocation process? In short, not easily. In fact, some of the pitfalls associated with trying to do this are classed under the general name of "Lord's Paradox."[7] That the difficulties of such an adjustment have acquired the description *paradox* reflects the subtle problems associated with trying to make causal inferences without true random assignment.

Thus it seems[8] that making most causal inferences within the context of VAM requires assumptions that are too heroic for realistic school situations, for they all require a control group that yields a plausible Y^*. Let me emphasize that the gain score itself cannot be interpreted as a causal effect unless you believe that without the specific treatment (Mr. Jones) the student's score at the end of the year would have been the same as it was at the beginning.

DEALING WITH MISSING OR ERRONEOUS DATA: THE SECOND CHALLENGE

The government [is] extremely fond of amassing
great quantities of statistics. These are raised to
the nth degree, the cube roots are extracted, and
the results are arranged into elaborate and impressive
displays. What must be kept ever in mind, however,
is that in every case, the figures are first put down
by a village watchman, and he puts down
anything he damn well pleases.
—Sir Josiah Charles Stamp (1880–1941)

To be able to partition student test score changes into pieces attributable to the district, the teacher, and the student requires data from other teachers within the district as well as the performance of the

---

to have that student placed in their class, one of them was unfortunate to get him or her, and hence that teacher's performance will look worse than it ought to without that bit of bad luck. This is but a single example of the possible problems that must be surmounted if student gain scores are to be successfully and fairly used to evaluate teachers.

[7] Lord 1967; Holland and Rubin 1983; Wainer 1991; Wainer and Brown 2004.

[8] Rubin, Stuart, and Zanutto 2004.

student with other teachers. Thus longitudinal data for each student is critical. But a district database compiled over time will generally have substantial missing data. Sometimes a score is missing; sometimes there is a missing link between a score and a teacher, sometimes background information has been omitted. Data can be missing because of student mobility (a student transfers in or out of the district), because of absenteeism on the day a test was administered, or because of clerical errors. There are many reasons. Before going into further details of the specific problems of missing data in the VAM context it seems useful to see some historic examples of how missing data, or more generally, nonrandomly selected data, can suggest incorrect inferences. Two of the examples I have chosen represent the findings of, first, a nineteenth-century Swiss physician and, second, a ninth-grade science project. My mentor, the Princeton polymath John Tukey, used to say that there were two kinds of lawyers: One tells you that you can't do it, the other tells you how to do it. To avoid being the wrong kind, the third example I present illustrates one way to draw correct inferences from a nonrandom sample with Abraham Wald's ingenious model for aircraft armoring.

Example 1: The Most Dangerous Profession

In 1835 the Swiss physician H. C. Lombard published the results of a study on the longevity of various professions. His data were very extensive, consisting of death certificates gathered over more than a half century in Geneva. Each certificate contained the name of the deceased, his profession, and age at death (a sample of Lombard's results translated into English is shown in table 9.1; the original French is in table 9.2, in the appendix to this chapter). Lombard used these data to calculate the mean longevity associated with each profession. Lombard's methodology was not original with him, but instead was merely an extension of a study carried out by R. R. Madden that was published two years earlier. Lombard found that the average age of death for the various professions mostly ranged from the early fifties to the midsixties. These were somewhat younger than those found by Madden, but this was expected since Lombard was dealing with ordinary people rather than the "geniuses" in Madden's (the positive correlation between fame and longevity was well known even

TABLE 9.1

Longevity for various professions in Geneva
(from 1776 until 1830)

Professions	Total number of deaths	Average longevity			
		Calculated on the total number of deaths	Calculated after eliminating violent deaths		
			Number of cases of violent death		Average longevity
			Suicide	*Accidental*	
Chocolate makers	9	73.6			73.6
Hosiery makers	38	69.0	1		69.1
Casters	47	59.4	1	3	60.4
Candy makers	28	55.2		2	57.1
Carpenters	176	55.1		12	55.7
Farmers	767	54.7	2	16	55.4
Shoemakers	376	54.2		5	54.4
Innkeepers	28	53.4		2	54.3
Butchers	77	53.0		3	53.1
Hat makers	39	50.9		2	51.6
Bakers	82	49.8		4	50.3
Enamel workers	75	48.7	2	5	49.7
Roofers	26	47.7		7	48.8
Barbers	16	47.4		1	49.3
Tinsmiths	39	45.6		4	47.0
Servants	177	45.4		7	46.0
Merchant's assistant	58	38.9	1	5	39.4
Students	39	20.2	1	3	20.7

Source: Lombard 1835.

then). But Lombard's study yielded one surprise; the most dangerous profession—the one with the shortest longevity—was that of "student" with an average age of death of only 20.7! Lombard recognized the reason for this anomaly, but apparently did not connect it to his other results.

Example 2: The Twentieth Century Was a Dangerous Time

In 1997, to revisit Lombard's methodology Samuel Palmer gathered 204 birth and death dates from the Princeton (NJ) Cemetery.[9] This

---

[9] Wainer, Palmer, and Bradlow 1998.

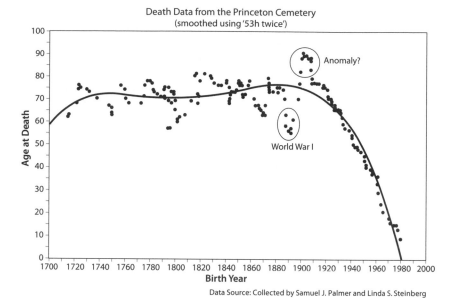

Figure 9.1. The longevities of 204 people buried in Princeton Cemetery shown as a function of the year of their birth. The data points were smoothed using "53h twice" (Tukey 1977), an iterative procedure of running medians.

cemetery opened in the mid-1700s, and has people buried in it born in the early part of that century. Those interred include Grover Cleveland, John Von Neumann, and Kurt Gödel.

When age at death was plotted as a function of birth year (after suitable smoothing to make the picture coherent)[10] we see the result shown as figure 9.1. We find that the age of death stays relatively constant until 1920, when the longevity of the people in the cemetery begins to decline rapidly. The average age of death decreases from around seventy years of age in the 1900s to as low as ten in the 1980s. It becomes obvious immediately that there must be a reason for the anomaly in the data (what we might call the "Lombard Surprise"), but what? Was it a

---

[10] The points shown in figure 9.1 are those generated by a nonlinear smoothing of the raw data. The smoother used was "53h-twice" (Tukey 1977), which involves taking running medians every 5, then running medians of those every 3, then a weighted linear combination. This smoothed estimate is then subtracted from the original data and the process repeated on the residuals. The resulting two smooths are then added together for the final estimate shown.

war or a plague that caused the rapid decline? Has a neonatal section been added to the cemetery? Was it only opened to poor people after 1920? None of these: the reason for the decline is nonrandom sampling. People cannot be buried in the cemetery if they are not already dead. Relatively few people born in the 1980s are buried in the cemetery and thus no one born in the 1980s who was found in Princeton Cemetery in 1997 could have been older than seventeen.

How can we draw valid inferences from nonrandomly sampled data? The answer is "not easily" and certainly not without risk. The only way to draw inferences is if we have a model for the mechanism by which the data were sampled. Let us consider one well-known example of such a model.

Example 3: Bullet Holes and a Model for Missing Data

The statistician Abraham Wald, in work during World War II was trying to determine where to add extra armor to planes on the basis of the pattern of bullet holes in returning aircraft.[11] His conclusion was to determine carefully where returning planes had been shot and *put extra armor every place else!*

Wald made his discovery by drawing an outline of a plane (crudely shown in figure 9.2 and then putting a mark on it where a returning aircraft had been shot. Soon the entire plane had been covered with marks except for a few key areas. It was at this point that he interposed a model for the missing data, the planes that did not return. He assumed that planes had been hit more or less uniformly, and hence those aircraft hit in the unmarked places had been unable to return, and thus were the areas that required more armor.

Wald's key insight was his model for the nonresponse. From his observation that planes hit in certain areas were still able to return to base, Wald inferred that the planes that didn't return must have been hit somewhere else. Note that if he used a different model analogous to "those lying within Princeton Cemetery have the same longevity as those without" (i.e., that the planes that returned were hit about the same as those that didn't return), he would have arrived at exactly the opposite (and wrong) conclusion.

---

[11] Mangel and Samaniego 1984; Wald 1980.

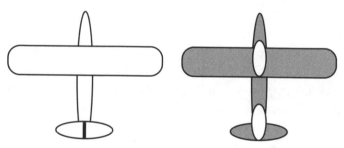

Figure 9.2. A schematic representation of Abraham Wald's ingenious scheme to investigate where to armor aircraft. The left figure shows an outline of a plane, the right shows the same plane
after the location of bullet holes was recorded.

To test Wald's model requires heroic efforts. Some of the planes that
did not return must be found, and the patterns of bullet holes in them
must be recorded. In short, to test the validity of Wald's model for missing data requires that we sample from the unselected population—we
must try to get a random sample, even if it is a small one. This strategy
remains the basis for the only empirical solution to making inferences
from nonrandom samples.

In the cemetery example if we want to get an unbiased estimate of
longevities, we might halt our data series at a birth date of 1900. Or we
might avoid the bias entirely by looking at longevity as a function of
death date rather than birth date.

These three examples are meant to illustrate how far wrong we can
go when data that are missing are assumed missing-at-random, that the
data that are not observed are just like the data that are observed. Yet
this is precisely what is commonly done with value-added models. Can
we believe that children who miss exams are just like those who show
up? That children who move into or out of the district are the same as
those who do neither? There is ample evidence that such assumptions
are very far from true.[12] It doesn't take much imagination to concoct a
plan for gaming the system that would boost a district's scores. For
example, during the day of the fall testing have a field trip for high-
scoring students; this will mean that the "pre" test scores will be artificially low, as the missing scores will be imputed from the scores that

[12] For example, Dunn, Kadane, and Garrow 2003.

were obtained. Thus when these higher-scoring students show up in the spring for the "post" test, an overlarge gain will be observed. Similarly, one could organize a spring field trip for the students who are expected to do poorly, and hence their "post" scores would be imputed too high. Or do both, for an even bigger boost. Of course sanctions against such shenanigans could be instituted, but clever people, when pressed, can be very inventive, especially when the obstacle to higher ratings for school performance is an unrealistic assumption about the missingness.

It is unknown how sensitive VAM parameter estimates are to missing data that are nonignorable, but ongoing research should have some empirical answers shortly.

I do not mean to suggest that it is impossible to gain useful insights from nonrandomly selected data; only that it is difficult and great care must be taken in drawing inferences. Remember James Thurber's fable of "The Glass in the Field" summarized in chapter 1. Thurber's moral, "He who hesitates is sometimes saved," is analogous to my main point: that a degree of safety can exist when one makes inferences from nonrandomly selected data, if those inferences are made with caution. Some simple methods are available that help us draw inferences when caution is warranted; they ought to be used.

This chapter is an inappropriate vehicle to discuss these special methods for inference in detail.[13] Instead let me describe the general character of any "solution." First, no one should be deluded and believe that unambiguous inferences can be made from a nonrandom sample. They can't. The magic of statistics cannot create information when there is none. We cannot know for sure the longevity of those who are still alive or the scores for those who didn't take the test. Any inferences that involve such information are doomed to be equivocal. What can we do? One approach is to make up data that might plausibly have come from the unsampled population (i.e., from some hypothesized model for selection) and include them with our sample as if they were real. Then see what inferences we would draw. Next make up some other data and see what inferences are suggested. Continue making up data until all plausible possibilities are covered. When this process is finished, see

---

[13] For such details the interested reader is referred to Little and Rubin 1987; Rosenbaum 1995; and Wainer 1986 for a beginning.

how stable are the inferences drawn over the entire range of these data imputations. The multiple imputations may not give a good answer, but they can provide an estimate of how sensitive inferences are to the unknown. If this is not done, you have not dealt with possible selection biases—you have only ignored them.

DO TESTS PROVIDE THE EVIDENCE FOR THE INFERENCES VAM WOULD HAVE US MAKE?

If you want to measure change you
should not change the measure.
—Albert Beaton and Rebecca Zwick

The wisdom of Beaton and Zwick's well-known epigram is obvious even to those without extensive psychometric training, yet the validity of most of the inferences from value-added models relies heavily on measures of change based on changing tests and changing constructs. Measuring academic progress is not like measuring height. What constitutes competent reading for a second-grader is quite different from that for a fifth-grader; and it is different in quality as well as general facility.[14] This point was elaborated on by Michigan statistician William Schmidt in 2004, when he examined the structure of Michigan's mathematics curriculum from second to eighth grade (summarized in figure 9.3). Schmidt looked at mathematics because he believed the strong hierarchical structure of the subject meant that it was more likely than other subjects to yield a set of coherent and meaningful change scores. He concluded that it did not; in his words, "Math is *not* math."

Schmidt found that the math curriculum's focus in early grades was on the concept and manipulation of numbers; as time went on it shifted, first toward issues in measurement and later toward algebra and geometry. Since sensible tests are aligned with the curriculum, the subject matter of the tests changed over time—even over a year or two. Hence his conclusion that just because you call what is being measured

---

[14] This point was made eloquently by Mark Reckase (2004).

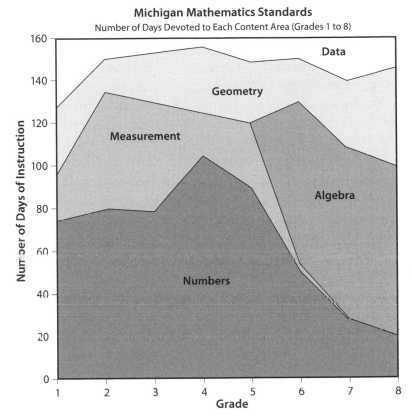

Figure 9.3. The amounts of time that the Michigan math curriculum standards suggest be spent on different components of math from first to eighth grade (from Schmidt 2004)

"math" in two different years does not mean that it is the same thing. But how are we to measure change if we insist on changing the measure? What are change scores measuring in such a circumstance?

This is the core question. What is a change score measuring when the construct underlying the measure changes in this fashion? In this instance it is some general underlying ability to do math. By far, the most common analytic result obtained by looking for the best single representation of performance underlying a broad range of cognitive measures is some measure of intelligence—usually called *g*. This is well described in hundreds of research reports spanning most of the twentieth century.[15] We shall not get into the extent to which this kind of ability is genetic, but it is well established that modifying such a derived trait is not easily done, and so it is a poor characteristic by which to weigh the efficacy of schooling. And this is the irony of VAM; by focusing attention on a change score over a multiyear period, VAM directs us away from those aspects of a child's performance that are most likely to inform us about the efficacy of that child's schooling.

The point is surely obvious, but for completeness, let me mention that this kind of value-added assessment is essentially worthless at making comparisons across subjects. It does not tell us how much of a gain in physics is equivalent to some fixed gain in Latin. The same issues that we discussed in earlier chapters are manifested here in spades. But because VAM software gives out numbers, unthinking users can be fooled into thinking that the magic of statistics has been able to answer questions that seem insoluble. It can't.

CONCLUSION

Good teachers understand the wisdom of a Talmudic midrash attributed to Rabban Yohanan ben Zakkai:

> If there be a plant in your hand when they say to you, Behold the Messiah!, go and plant the plant, and afterward go out to greet him.

The educational establishment regularly discovers new sources of redemption—this year's promise is that value-added assessment will save us all—but one suspects that the Lord is best served by teachers who find salvation in the routine transactions of their daily work. Value-added assessment may yet help us in this task, but there are many challenges yet to overcome before these models are likely to help us with the very difficult questions VAM was formulated to answer. In this chapter I have chosen what I believe are the three major issues that need much more work:

---

[15] The work of Ree and Earles (1991a; 1991b; 1992; 1993), which summarizes a massive amount of work in this area done by military researchers, is but one example; Jensen (1998) provides an encyclopedic description.

1. Assessing the causal effect of specific teachers on the changes observed in their students
2. A more realistic treatment of missing data
3. Standardizing and stabilizing the outcome measures used to measure gains.

There are others.

Appendix

TABLE 9.2
Sur la durée de la vie dans diverses professions a Genève
(depuis 1776 à 1830)

Professions	Nombre total des morts	Vie Moyenne Calculée sur le nom. tot. des morts	Vie Moyenne Calculée en défalquant les mort violentes — Nombre de cas de mort violentes — Volontaire	Accidentelle	Vie Moyenne
Chocolatiers	9	73.6			73.6
Faiseurs de bas	38	69.0	1		69.1
Fondeurs	47	59.4	1	3	60.4
Confiseurs	28	55.2		2	57.1
Charpentiers	176	55.1		12	55.7
Agriculteurs	267	54.7	2	16	55.4
Cordonniers	376	54.2		5	54.4
Encaveurs	28	53.4		2	54.3
Bouchers	77	53.0		3	53.1
Chapeliers	39	50.9		2	51.6
Boulangers	82	49.8		4	50.3
Emailleurs	75	48.7	2	5	49.7
Couvreurs	26	47.7		7	48.8
Barbiers	16	47.4		1	49.3
Ferblantiers	39	45.6		4	47.0
Domestiques	177	45.4		7	46.0
Commis-négocians	58	38.9	1	5	39.4
Etudiants	39	20.2	1	3	20.7

Source: Lombard 1835.

10

❧ ❧

Shopping for Colleges When
What We Know Ain't

What we don't know won't hurt us,
it's what we do know that ain't.
—Will Rogers

Will Rogers's well-known aphorism came to mind as I was reading
a report by Eric Dash in the *New York Times*[1] on a new and improved
method for ranking colleges and universities, developed by Christopher Avery and his colleagues. Automobile commercials often tell us
that we must choose cars wisely since, after a new home, it is the most
expensive purchase we will make. And, because of this cost there are an
unending number of reports comparing and measuring every aspect of
each year's crop of new vehicles, using a range of criteria from *Consumer
Reports'* practical ones (comfort, reliability, safety) to the various enthu-
siast magazines that focus more on performance and aesthetics. But is
the purchase of a car really the second most expensive thing we spend
money on? Having just received a bill for $25,000 for one semester of
my son's college expenses (and having already paid one just like it for
the first semester), I doubted it. Indeed, if you have enough children,

This chapter developed from H. Wainer, "Shopping for Colleges When What We
Know Ain't," *Journal of Consumer Research*, 32(3) (2005): 337–342.

[1] October 20, 2004. I would like to thank my wife, Linda Steinberg, who left Dash's
article laid out on the breakfast table with the telling accusation, "They ignored early
admission!" Were it not for her sharp eyes and keen intellect, I would almost certainly
have missed it.

education expenses can easily top the cost of a home. I suspect that medical costs (including the partially unseen monthly contributions for insurance paid by one's employer) also dwarf car payments.

Yet how much help does a consumer get in making education and health care decisions? By my reckoning, when compared with the information available about cars, not much. Atul Gawande in the December 6, 2004, issue of the *New Yorker* wrote an essay entitled "The Bell Curve," in which he reported, apparently with surprise, that all centers for the treatment of cystic fibrosis did not yield equally good outcomes. In fact the outcomes (mean age of death) varied in a bell-shaped curve. What was surprising was the amount of variability of the distribution (results varied from a mean survival age in the twenties to well beyond forty) and also the attitudes of the workers in each of the centers—they all thought they were doing a good job. If the doctors working within the centers don't have the information to make an informed, accurate judgment, how can potential consumers of their services?

And so what about judging the quality of undergraduate education? The cost of an undergraduate degree at a private university has historically been approximately equal to that of one new car per year—it used to be a Ford, but is currently about that of an E-class Mercedes. But instead of trading it in each year, it is roughly equivalent to buying a new Mercedes and at the end of each year shoving it over a cliff and buying another one. In view of these costs you would think that there would be extensive, empirically based help to aid consumers in their choice. Instead we have the annual *U.S. News and World Report* rankings (hereafter USN&WR), based on a mixture of variables weighted in a somewhat ad hoc manner. The variables used in this well-known index are all related in some deep conceptual way to the quality of education (e.g., student/faculty ratio, endowment per pupil). Unfortunately, some of the component variables of this index can be manipulated by the institution. For example, the "yield," the proportion of students admitted who choose to attend, can be manipulated by increasing the number of students admitted through binding early decision. But despite these flaws, the USN&WR does seem to reflect generally the consensus of opinion about the quality of colleges and universities (although the absence of the great public universities (e.g., Berkeley, Michigan, Wisconsin, Illinois, UCLA) from the top rankings suggests that some aspect of those rankings needs tweaking.

USN&WR rankings do not include expert opinion, except as experts choose the variables to be used. Might this aid in providing a truer description? Perhaps, although it is hard for me to understand who would qualify as an expert, and where the experts would get their special information. I remember a few years ago looking at peer rankings of graduate departments and being delighted to discover that among statistics departments my own alma mater was in the top ten (although my trust in the process was tempered by the knowledge that, despite its lofty ranking, Princeton's statistics department had been disbanded decades earlier).

Thus the combination of an obvious great need for good information to aid consumers in what is likely one of the largest of life's expenditures along with the suspicion that the existing indices of quality were lacking some important aspects of schools, led me to read Dash's report of a new and improved ranking with great interest.

Dash summarized the results provided in detail in a technical report by four distinguished researchers.[2] Their approach was to develop a preference ranking based on college applicants who were accepted into two or more colleges. They viewed applicants' decisions about where to attend as a sequence of binary choices in which they preferred the one they decided to attend over each of the others that had accepted them. And, by viewing the entire set of choices as a kind of complex experimental design,[3] the researchers could link the various schools through the latticework of application and acceptance choices that all of the students had made. Through this method they were able to place all the institutions onto a single, common scale.[4] An undeniably clever approach, but what does it get us?

I will not discuss the shortcomings of their sample, and the biases that that might yield, for if the methodology is sound, future samples could be drawn that were large enough and broad enough to allow the inferences of interest. Let us instead consider the heart of the methodology. First, what does it purport to measure? Is it the quality of the schools or their programs? No. The authors are quite clear in this and tell us that it is a preference ranking and only tells us how the applicants

[2] Avery et al. 2004.
[3] An incomplete Block Design.
[4] They used a variant of a Luce-Bradley-Terry model (Luce 1959).

view their options. Is this helpful knowledge? How would we feel if *Consumer Reports* only told us how many people preferred one car to another, without telling us why? And how useful would this be if we found out that all of the people who made this judgment did so before they owned either car?

I will leave a deeper discussion of this issue to other accounts, for now it seems more important to examine the validity of the methodology Avery et al. used in calculating their preference rankings. The biggest flaw in their methodology, it seems to me, is their treatment of missing data. Missing data is an enormous problem in all observational studies[5] (remember the brief discussion in chapter 9 on the effect of missing data on teacher evaluations using value-added methodology), and its pernicious effects enter into this problem in an interesting way.

Avery et al. suggest that by using a preference ranking they eliminate many of the possible ways that schools can manipulate the rankings. That may be, but in doing so they introduce a bias that may be so large as to sink the entire enterprise. Specifically what do you do about students who only apply to one school? One might assume that these students have a very strong preference for that school—indeed so strong that they would choose it over all others; or at least over all others that are likely to admit them. If the preference of such strong supporters of a particular institution were not to be counted, it would surely bias the rankings of that institution downward, yet that is exactly what Avery et al. do. They treat any student who applies to just one institution as missing data—indeed missing-at-random. What the assumption of missing-at-random means is that the preferences of these students are assumed to be just the same as those who applied to more than one institution. While such an assumption makes computation easy, in this instance at least, it stretches the bounds of credulity.

How much does this assumption affect the outcome? If only a very small percentage of an entering class fall into the category of applying to just one school, the effect, though likely in one direction, will be proportionally small. Moreover, if all schools in the same stratum of desirability have about the same rate of special fans, one might make up an

---

[5] See Rosenbaum 2002 for a lucid description of what can be done; Little and Rubin 1987 for a more general discussion of dealing with missing data; and Wainer 1986 for a lively discussion on the impact of missing data on inferences.

argument that the bias is spread around, more or less equally, and so the preference rankings are still okay. Unfortunately neither of these possibilities is true—not by a long shot.

Many (but not all) of the most famous colleges and universities in the United States have a policy of early admission. This policy is aimed at making life easier for both the applying students and for the institution. For those students who can decide early in their senior year in high school what college they would most like to attend (always with the caveat that it is among those schools likely to admit them), they can apply early. But they can only apply to that one place, and with the proviso that if they are accepted they will definitely attend. The college then responds, usually before the end of December. There is also the suggestion that students' chances of acceptance are greater under early admission than they would be if they were included in the regular process. So, in addition to getting the angst of the admission process over early, the student gains an advantage. The institution gains by making the composition of its freshman class more certain, and, perhaps incidentally, boosting its yield statistic in the USN&WR rankings. Surely a win-win proposition. But none of these avid supporters of a particular institution get their affection counted in the Avery et al. preference rankings.

How popular is early admission? I haven't made an exhaustive study, but more than a third of Princeton and Penn's 2005 freshman class were early admission, as were more than 30 percent of Duke's. So the idea that only a handful applies to just one school is clearly wrong. But is the same bias spread more or less equally across all schools? Alas, no.

Some schools have adopted a procedure commonly dubbed "early action" that is just like early decision except that the applicant is not obligated to attend. It is supposed (I have no data) that this provides applicants with the same early decision boost in the likelihood of acceptance, but with a little more leeway. What I suspect happens is that some students who are accepted under early action never apply anywhere else, but some others do. They might do this for ego boosting, to try for other schools that might be more of a reach, or to gather other aid packages to be used to negotiate a better deal with their first choice. Whatever the motivation or strategy, schools with early action have a cohort of strong fans with the opportunity to apply elsewhere, and

TABLE 10.1
Two Sets of College Rankings

U.S. News and World Report 2004 college survey	Avery et al. Rankings 2000 high school senior survey
1 Princeton	1 Harvard
Harvard	2 Yale
3 Yale	3 Stanford
4 University of Pennsylvania	4 Cal Tech
5 Duke	5 MIT
MIT	6 Princeton
Stanford	7 Brown
8 Cal Tech	8 Columbia
9 Columbia	9 Amherst
Dartmouth	10 Dartmouth
11 Northwestern	11 Wellesley
Washington University (St. Louis)	12 University of Pennsylvania
13 Brown	13 Notre Dame
14 Cornell	14 Swarthmore
Johns Hopkins	15 Cornell
University of Chicago	16 Georgetown
17 Rice	17 Rice
18 Notre Dame	18 Williams
Vanderbilt	19 Duke
20 Emory	20 University of Virginia

hence be counted in the preference ranking. This opportunity is denied those strongest supporters of schools with early decision.

Table 10.1 compares the top USN&WR rankings and the top Avery rankings. We see the now expected results that the five highest ranked schools are all early action schools, whereas Princeton (moved from first to sixth), Penn (from fourth to twelfth), and Duke (from fifth to nineteenth) are all early decision schools. Clearly ignoring data missing in this way yields serious consequences. How can we correct this flaw? Avery et al. recognized that missing data were a serious problem. They chose a traditional econometric approach to deal with it; they decided to hypothesize a model for the missingness, and thence treat the model as if it were true. The model they chose was to assume that the unobserved data, the preferences that would have been observed had students who applied to only one school applied to others, would have yielded the same preference ranking as the one calculated from the observed data. In short, they decided to treat the unobserved data as if they were missing-at-random. This option is surely not the only choice, nor, I posit, the most likely.

How large an effect can nonrandomly gathered data yield in practical circumstances? We are all aware of various kinds of call-in or Internet surveys in which convenience samples are used to provide an estimate of the popularity of a product, a candidate, or a policy. Invariably the caveat is offered that this is not a "scientifically designed" survey, but the results are then discussed as if they were meaningful anyway. Such an attitude much more often than not takes us down a path of mistaken inferences. As a way of illustrating just how profound an effect self-selection can have on our inferences, remember the three examples in chapter 9, Lombard's most dangerous profession, Princeton Cemetery, and Wald's airplane armoring.

There are many other examples of situations in which self-selection anomalies arise. Four of these are:

1. In 100 autopsies, a significant relationship was found between age at death and the length of the lifeline on the palm.[6] Actually what was discovered was that wrinkles and old age go together.
2. In 90 percent of all deaths resulting from barroom brawls, the victim was the one who instigated the fight. One questions the wit of the remaining 10 percent who didn't point at the body on the floor when the police asked, "Who started this?"
3. In March 1991, the *New York Times* reported the results of data gathered by the American Society of Podiatry that stated that 88 percent of all women wear shoes at least one size too small. Who would be most likely to participate in such a poll?
4. In testimony before a February 1992 meeting of a committee of the Hawaii State Senate, then considering a law requiring all motorcyclists to wear a helmet, one witness declared that despite having been in several accidents during his twenty years of motorcycle riding, a helmet would not have prevented any of the injuries he received. Who was unable to testify? Why?

[6] Newrick, Affie, and Corrall 1990.

An analysis of the sensitivity of inferences to the model of missing data employed can be accomplished easily by simply using a variety of plausible models for the missing data and seeing how much our inferences change depending on the choice of model. In the specific instance of college preferences, there are some obvious alternative models to the "missing at random" model that Avery et al. employed. One extreme imputation would be to assume that everyone who applied to only one school would have preferred that school to all others (probably just as wrong as missing-at-random). After imputing this into the analysis, we could examine how much the preference rankings have changed. If they remained essentially the same (as would be the case if very few data were missing), we could feel a little more confident in our rankings. If there were profound changes, we should begin to feel nervous. We might then substitute various other models for missingness—I leave it to the imagination of the reader how to construct them.[7] The key idea here is that while multiple imputations may not give a good answer, they can provide an estimate of how sensitive inferences are to the unknown. If we do not do this, we have ignored any possible selection biases.

Bottom Line

Despite noble efforts, I fear that the solution to ranking colleges still lies out of reach—or at least it is unreached so far. USN&WR rankings, based on plausible, objective criteria, are the best we have so far. This is not an endorsement, for as we have seen (e.g., here and in chapter 7) some of the variables USN&WR uses can be manipulated (yields through early admission, and mean SAT through making admission tests optional). But the difficulty of trying to rank schools, when so much background information is publicly available, makes clearer how hard it is to compare students for whom so much is hidden.

---

[7] Although an iterative one in which all single school applicants prefer their school to all others except the top k schools, where k is a parameter to be varied and what is top is iteratively determined, seems to capture much of the spirit of the procedure I am endorsing here. One could then summarize the results of multiple imputations as a graph that shows the variability of the rankings as a function of k.

11

⤳ ⤳

Of CATs and Claims

The First Step toward Wisdom

The first step toward wisdom is calling
things by their right names.
—Confucius

I've got a little CAT,
And I'm very fond of that.
—Joseph Tabrar, 1892

The goal of this book parallels the principal goal of much of science—
to try to understand the world through the integration of evidence
and careful thought. I would like to end with a brief discussion of one
instance where this tactic, which has always seemed completely convincing to me, was an utter failure in convincing some others. Such fail-
ures occur, alas, with disheartening frequency. A majority of this book
has tried to establish that anecdotes are not data, and so basing decisions on anecdotes yields no guarantee of a positive outcome. As part
of this chapter I try to go one step further and emphasize an important,
but too rarely recognized, distinction between data and evidence. One
might say, "I believe that you'll have a nice birthday, but my belief is
not supported by any data." Of course there is likely lots of data; the

This chapter developed from H. Wainer, "Some Practical Considerations When Converting a Linearly Administered Test to an Adaptive Format," *Educational Measurement:
Issues and Practice* 12 (1): 15–20, 1993.

temperature, the Yankee's team batting average, my blood sugar level. What I mean is, "My belief is not supported by any *evidence.*"

Evidence is data related to a claim. If I want to establish a claim regarding your facility in French, I could record your shoe size and Social Security number—these are undoubtedly data—but they are not evidence. To illustrate this distinction on a topic relevant to this book's theme, I will take the opportunity to introduce you to a modern marvel of measurement, Computerized adaptive testing, in which the test shapes itself to suit the examinee. It is in the use of this technology that an instance of confusion between data and evidence emerges. But I am getting ahead of myself; let me begin at the beginning.

THE SHIFTING CHARACTER OF TESTING FROM INDIVIDUAL TO GROUP ADMINISTRATIONS

The use of tests to improve the use of human resources is very old indeed, with recorded instances ranging back to China's Xia dynasty more than 4,000 years ago. But the beginning of the twentieth century saw a shift in the way tests were administered. For most of testing's history the majority of examinations were given one-on-one by a wise examiner and a nervous candidate. This began to change in the nineteenth-century Indian civil service exams instituted under the British Raj, but accelerated when the military needed to classify large numbers of enlisted men in a short time at modest cost. After World War I, the mass-administered examination became the dominant form.

A mass-administered exam had many advantages. It was much cheaper and easier to administer, especially after the technology of multiple-choice items was mastered. Also, because its content could be carefully scrutinized and standardized, it was fairer and vastly more reliable. And because each test item took a relatively small amount of time to administer, a much broader span of topics could be covered, thus minimizing the possibility that an unfortunate choice of topics for the exam would disadvantage examinees whose instruction offered a slightly different view of the subject matter.

SHORTCOMINGS OF GROUP ADMINISTRATIONS

But group administration also had some drawbacks. The most important one was efficiency for the individual examinee. When a test is
individually administered the examiner doesn't waste time asking
inappropriate questions. If a question is clearly too hard we learn nothing when the examinee gets it wrong; similarly, if a question is too easy.
We get maximal information from a question that is aimed close to the
examinee's ability. A mass-administered standardized test must be constructed for the ability distribution of the anticipated population, with
most of its items in the middle of the difficulty range and relatively
fewer at the extremes. Thus the examinees whose abilities are near the
middle are most accurately measured, whereas those at the extremes
much less so. This issue becomes critical for diagnostic testing in which
we wish to use the performance on the test to guide further instruction.
An individualized exam can zero in on the examinee's weaknesses and
pinpoint areas for remediation. A mass-administered exam would need
to become impractically long to yield equivalent results.

CATS: A COMPROMISE

All this changed in the latter part of the twentieth century as computers
moved out of climate-controlled rooms and onto everyone's desktop.
A new form of testing was developed called a Computerized Adaptive
Test, or CAT for short.[1]

A CAT tries to emulate a wise examiner. In a CAT the examinee sits
in front of a computer monitor and the testing algorithm begins the
test by selecting an item of moderate difficulty from a large pool of test
items. These items had been constructed previously to span the entire
range of examinee abilities. If the examinee gets the item right the CAT
algorithm chooses a more difficult one; if the examinee gets it wrong it
selects an easier one. This continues until the algorithm has zeroed in
on the examinee's ability with as much accuracy as required. Typically,

---

[1] The standard reference for CAT is Wainer 2000.

this takes about half as many items as would be required for a linearly administered paper-and-pencil test.

Of course, the item selection is more complicated than this. The algorithm must also choose items that cover all of the aspects of the topic being covered by the exam, and it tries to use all items at each difficulty level equally. Reasons for the former restriction are obvious, for the latter it is for test security. Because computers are more expensive than #2 pencils, CATs are typically administered a few at a time, continuously. This is in sharp contrast to gathering hundreds of examinees together in a school gymnasium on a specific Saturday in October and passing out test books, answer sheets, and #2 pencils. Continuous test administrations open wider the doors to cheating through item pilferage, hence the need for large item pools in which all of the items of the same difficulty level are used with more or less equal frequency.

A CAT is scored differently than a linear test. Because all examinees correctly answer approximately 50 percent of the items presented to them, the old scoring standby "percentage correct" is meaningless. Instead we must use something akin to "the difficulty of the hardest items answered correctly consistently." Or, more metaphorically, think of the test items as a sequence of hurdles of increasing heights. A typical response pattern would yield a series of low hurdles (easy items) left standing and a sequence of high hurdles (hard items) knocked over. The examinee's ability is measured in the same metric as the height of the hurdles, and it lies between the height of the highest hurdle cleared and the height of the lowest hurdle knocked over. If an examinee answers all items asked of her correctly, all we can say for sure is that her ability is greater than the difficulty of the most difficult item presented.

CATS CAN DO A LOT, BUT NOT EVERYTHING

When CATs were first introduced we were all delighted with what could be done.

1. Individuals can work at their own pace, and speed of response can be recorded as additional information.

2. Each individual can stay busy productively—everyone is challenged but not discouraged.
3. The test can be scored immediately.
4. A greater variety of questions can be included, expanding the test developer's repertoire beyond multiple-choice questions.
5. Any errors uncovered in the test's items can be corrected on-the-fly, and hence the number of examinees exposed to the flawed item can be limited.

But some benefits of linear testing were lost. For example, you cannot review previously answered items and change your answer. Because the efficiency of the test depends on selecting an appropriate item after observing your response, if you change that response the item selected is no longer optimal. Skipping items, either with the notion of coming back to them later, or just going on and seeing what comes next, is no longer acceptable, because the item selection algorithm doesn't know what to do next. Thus, if you omit an item, your response must be treated as incorrect.

DOING IT ANYWAY: THE TRIUMPH OF HOPE OVER LOGIC

The problem is never how to get new,
innovative thoughts into your mind,
but how to get old ones out.
—Dee Hock, founder and former
CEO of VISA International

In a pair of articles published in 1992 and 1994, Mary Lunz and her colleagues asserted that "the opportunity to review items and alter responses is important to examinees," that they "feel at a disadvantage when they cannot review and alter their responses," and that "the security of a final review can provide comfort and reassurance to the examinee." They looked into allowing examinees some control over their exam by allowing them to skip an item they didn't want to answer. If an item was skipped, another one was chosen from the pool on the same topic and at about the same difficulty. Lunz et al. described experimental results that suggested that allowing examinees this sort of freedom had only a small effect on the outcome and hence recommended that operational tests consider including this additional flexibility.

Let us consider each of these ideas.

First, skipping: Consider a spelling test with a corpus of, say, 200,000 words. If I asked you to spell 100 words that I had chosen at random and you spelled 80 of them correctly I could safely infer that you could spell roughly 80 percent of the words in the corpus. But suppose after I asked you a word, you could choose to skip it and its successors until I offered a word that was more to your liking. And we continued doing this until you accepted 100 words (perhaps it took 1,000 words to arrive at these 100). Now if you spelled 100 of these correctly what could we infer about your spelling ability? All we can be sure of is that you could spell at least 100 words out of the corpus. The difference between these two tests—with and without skipping—is what statisticians characterize as the difference between *ignorable missingness* and *nonignorable missingness*. In the first case your nonresponses to the 199,900 words that I didn't ask you about can be ignored, because I know why you didn't respond—I didn't ask them. But in the second case your nonresponse to the 900 that you refused to answer cannot be ignored, because I don't know why you didn't answer. I might infer that you didn't try to spell them because you didn't know how, but even that isn't sure. So all that allowing skipping gets us is an increase in the uncertainty about the meaning of the test score.

Second, item review: Allowing item review can be benign, if an examinee doesn't change very many responses, or if the responses that are changed occurred toward the end of the test when her ability had already been pretty well estimated. But if she decides to revise the answers to items at the very beginning of the test, there could be a more profound effect. In addition, since most tests that allow review and revision of answers do so only after the test has been completed, revision of responses must diminish the efficiency of the sequence of items that were chosen to be presented to the examinee. Thus the accuracy of the final score will be diminished. Whether this inaccuracy is of serious consequence depends on many factors. But neither accuracy nor efficiency is our primary concern, for minor variations from optimality yields only minor effects.

Our concern is with the consequences of using the flexibility provided by these well-intentioned deviations from proper procedure to
game the system.

GATHERING DATA, BUT NOT EVIDENCE

The desire to keep the old procedures within the new format was
remarkably strong. Hence there were dozens of studies[2] measuring
the effect of allowing skipping and revision in a CAT. Many of these
studies were extensive and careful with control groups, random assignment, and all of the other features that characterize the gold standard of
science. And these studies provided data that supported the notion that
examinees who made only modest use of these extra freedoms would
not change their final scores very much.

But are these data evidence? To answer this question, we must make
explicit exactly what are the claims that these data were gathered to
support. As I discussed in chapter 6, tests can have three purposes:

1. Tests as measurements
2. Tests as prods
3. Tests as contests

When tests are used for measurement, as they usually are to guide
decisions of placement or instruction, there is little incentive to cheat.
For if you score higher than you deserve, you might end up in a too
difficult course or missing out on some needed remediation. No sane
person cheats on an eye test.

When a test is a prod; for example giving a test to get students to
study, cheating may be a sensible strategy depending on what are the
consequences of the score.

But when tests are contests, where the higher scorer wins a job, gets
a license, earns a scholarship, or is offered entry into an elite school,
cheating may have practical value. This value may overwhelm the
legal, moral, and ethical strictures against it.

---

[2] See Vispoel 1998 for a thorough and accurate summary of this work.

And so the data generated by the studies that examine how moderate use of the freedom to skip items and change answers provides evidence supporting claims about the use of CATs for measurement. But what about for contests?

GAMING THE SYSTEM

Alas, for those examinees who decide to the game the system, these modifications make it easier. Consider the situation where a test is used for licensure. This is high-stakes indeed, for if you pass, you can practice your profession, whereas if you fail, you cannot. So the goal of the examinee is to get a score above some established standard. If the standard is high relative to an examinee's knowledge, is there a strategy that can be followed to increase her chances of passing?

Suppose someone follows the following four steps:

1. Never answer a question whose answer you do not know (keep skipping until you get one you know).
2. If you know the answer, be sure to choose an incorrect response. The item selection algorithm will then provide you with an easier one.
3. Continue with this until the testing session is complete. With the full assistance of the item selection machinery, you should have then received the easiest test that could be built from the item pool.
4. Use the opportunity to review your responses to change the answers to all items so that they are all correct.

Now comes the fun. Depending on the scoring method used, you will either be given a passing score (remember that if you get all items right, all that can be said of your ability is that it is greater than the most difficult item asked), or you get to smirk in court as the testing company tries to explain to a judge how it could fail someone who answered correctly every question he was asked. I imagine somewhere in the cross-examination the testing company will explain that you failed because you only answered easy questions, to which you can respond, "But those were the only questions you asked me."

This illustrates my point that data gathered to study these two kinds of modifications to CATs provides no evidence regarding claims when there is a real incentive to game the system. An experiment that would provide such evidence might use some examinees whose abilities are just below the passing standard and ask them to try this strategy and count how many of them can work it to a successful conclusion.

Of course one needn't be this extreme to game the system. There are many other possible strategies. For example, if, after you answer an item, the next one seems clearly easier, you can conclude you made a mistake and change your answer. But expanding on ways to beat the system is not my point. It is enough to show that by deviating from the "rules" of CAT you get into trouble. Some sources of trouble might be foreseeable and perhaps mitigated, but some surely will not be.

WHERE ARE WE NOW?

Don't worry about people stealing your ideas.
If your ideas are any good, you'll have
to ram them down people's throats.
—Howard Aiken[3]

Proposals for stretching the rules for CATs were made in 1992. In 1993 I laid out how those stretches could allow a motivated examinee to game the system. This warning did not deter large numbers of testing specialists from recommending these changes or from publishing irrelevant studies purportedly showing that such strategies were unlikely to have large effects. In the more than seventeen years since, published studies are still appearing[4] that offer suggestions on minimizing the potential damage. Too often data, but not evidence, are offered in support.

Old theories never die, just the people who believe them.

—Albert Einstein

---

[3] Howard Hathaway Aiken (1900–1973) was a pioneer in computing, being the primary engineer behind IBM's Harvard Mark I computer.

[4] A recent instance by Papanastasiou and Reckase (2007) tries to provide a workaround to help mitigate the damage. I remain convinced that the best strategy is to avoid the problem rather than to try to repair its damage.

Epilogue

I began this book with an observation by Richard Feynman, one of the twentieth century's most revered scientists.

> It doesn't matter how beautiful your theory is, it doesn't matter how smart you are. If it doesn't agree with experiment, it's wrong.

It seems to me that I am unlikely to go wrong ending with some allied observations.

The title of this book was chosen purposely to be evocative; when we make guesses about how to improve any complex process—and education certainly falls into that category—we ought to use evidence to guide our guesswork. Such guesses I would class as "educated." Then after we make those guesses we must subject them to careful scrutiny, both empirical and logical. And if the outcomes observed, after suitable checking to assure that all intervening steps are correct, are not what we expected, the guess was wrong. This emphasizes one consequence of the decision to use evidence as the deciding factor—evidence, not expert opinion. Once again, Richard Feynman:

> Science is the belief in the ignorance of experts.

I recognize that the decision to base actions on evidence is a tough one. In the last year we have seen how people armed with anecdotes, but not data, attacked evidence-based advice about who should have mammograms. Indeed many of the anecdotes relied on emotional counterfactual statements for their validity: "If my sister had not had a mammogram, she would not be alive today" or "If she had a mammogram, she would be alive today." The fact that such logically weak argumentation yielded almost immediate equivocation from government officials attests to how difficult it is to use the logical weight of evidence over the emotional power of anecdote. We must always remember that the plural of *anecdote* is not *data*.

The battle opposing emotion and anecdote against logic and evidence makes for fine theater—witness how popular were the inevitable showdowns between Mr. Spock's Vulcan logic and Captain Kirk's human emotion. I have argued that for setting policy or for making triage decisions in the face of scarce resources, we do far better using evidence. My role in this parallels Spock's when he explained, "Nowhere am I so desperately needed as among a shipload of illogical humans."[1]

This book is dedicated to demonstrating how evidence can be used to cast light on important issues, many of which are still under consideration. My concern, which led to the preparation of this book, was that despite counterevidence, various proposals for change in educational practice now gaining momentum are likely to be put into practice. I hope that the results of the mini-experiment provided by Bowdoin's experience in making the SAT optional will lead to a larger-scale examination of that logically and empirically flawed proposal. The formal adoption of a policy to evaluate teachers through the average change in test scores of their students was finalized in the Tennessee legislature in April 2010, and seems close to implementation in many other states. This idea sounds sensible if said quickly, but when examined more carefully we find that it is not ready for prime time. Some version might be useful in the future, but not yet.

All of this brings me to the topic of hubris. On these pages I have railed against those who advocate changes to the status quo without the support of empirical evidence to show that the changes would improve matters. This represents two different kinds of hubris: theirs in thinking that they are wiser than their predecessors whose work has yielded the current system, and mine in suggesting that their ideas are wrongheaded.

Their hubris first. We are not any smarter than those who have come before us. If we can make improvements, it is only because we have the benefit of additional experience—more evidence. In any complex operation, whether it is a manufacturing process or an educational system, there is always room for improvement. Yet how are we to reach the future? Experience has taught us a great deal about what kinds of optimization methods work in complex systems and what kinds do not. An almost surefire path to failure is to convene a blue-ribbon

[1] Spock in "I, Mudd."

committee with a title like "Education 2020" whose mandate is to pon-
der existing problems and come out with recommendations for the
future system. It doesn't work because even all-stars aren't that smart.
What does work is the implementation of constant experimentation, in
which small changes[2] are made to the process. Then the effects of the
changes are assessed. If the process improves, the size of the changes
is increased and the outcome monitored. If the process gets worse, the
changes are reversed and another variable is manipulated. Gradually,
the entire complex process moves toward optimization. If we follow
this approach, when the future arrives, the system of the future is there
to greet it. Critical to such an approach working are well-defined and
well-measured outcome variables so that we know what "improved"
means. We also need to understand enough about the process to be
able to select what are the most likely parameters, those whose change
would affect the outcome variable, and so guide the experimental
manipulations. It is on these two aspects that blue-ribbon panels may
be useful—and to lend political legitimacy to the entire enterprise.

Underlying the success of such an approach is the epistemological
belief that evidence, and not the power of authority or faith, must guide
change.

Now my hubris in making these suggestions: To write a book requires
the sustained belief that your thoughts and findings are of interest and
value to others. The sin of pride must be the one common trait that runs
through all authors. In my own defense note that my recommendations
are not based on any misplaced notion of my own special genius, but
rather on the much more pedestrian collecting of facts over a lifetime
of work. Thus, the frequency with which I write books has increased
with my years.

Marcel Proust likened aging to being "perched upon living stilts that
keep on growing"—thus we can see further as we age, but passage is
increasingly wobbly. This book is a testament to that process.

---

[2] "Small changes" can be small in the size of the change (like increasing the school year
by a few days) or small in the number units involved (trying it out at just a few carefully
chosen schools).

References

Angoff, W. H. 1972. A technique for the investigation of cultural differences. Paper presented at the meeting of the American Psychological Association, Honolulu. ERIC Document Reproduction Service No. ED 069686.

Angoff, W. H., and L. L. Cook. 1988. *Equating the Scores of the Prueba de Aptitud Academica and the Scholastic Aptitude Test.* College Board Report No. 88-2. New York: College Entrance Examination Board.

Angoff, W. H., and C. C. Modu. 1973. *Equating the Scales of the Prueba de Aptitud Academica and the Scholastic Aptitude Test.* Research Report 3. New York: College Entrance Examination Board.

Avery, C., M. Glickman, C. Hoxby, and A. Metrick. 2004. A revealed preference ranking of U.S. colleges and universities. NBER Working Paper No. 10803. Cambridge, MA: National Bureau of Economic Research.

Ballou, D., W. Sanders, and P. Wright. 2004. Controlling for student background in value-added assessment of teachers. *Journal of Educational and Behavioral Statistics* 29 (1): 37–65.

Beaton, A. E., and R. Zwick. 1990. *Disentangling the NAEP 1985–86 Reading Anomaly.* Princeton, NJ: Educational Testing Service.

Beller, M., N. Gafni, and P. Hanani. 2005. Constructing, adapting, and validating admissions tests in multiple languages: The Israeli case. In R. K. Hambleton, P. Merenda, and C. Spielberger, eds., *Adapting Educational and Psychological Tests for Cross-Cultural Assessment.* Hillsdale, NJ: Erlbaum, 297–319.

Bracey, G. W. 1991. Why can't they be like we were? *Phi Delta Kappan* 73:104–117.

———. 1998. The eighth Bracey report on the condition of public education. *Phi Delta Kappan* 80:112–131.

Bradlow, E. T., H. Wainer, and X. Wang. 1999. A Bayesian random effects model for testlets. *Psychometrika* 64:153–168.

Brigham, C. C. 1934. *The Reading of the Comprehensive Examination in English.* Princeton, NJ: Princeton University Press.

Camara, W. J. 1997. *The Relationship of PSAT/NMSQT Scores and AP Examination Grades.* Research Note RN-02. New York: The College Board, Office of Research and Development.

Camara, W. J., and R. Millsap. 1998. *Using the PSAT/NMSQT and Course Grades in Predicting Success in the Advanced Placement Program.* College Board Report No. 98-4. New York: The College Board.

Carson, C. C., R. M. Huelskamp, and T. D. Woodall. 1993. Perspectives on education in America. *Journal of Educational Research* 86:259–311.

Cizek, G. J. 1993. Rethinking psychometricians' beliefs about learning. *Educational Researcher* 22:4–9.

College Entrance Examination Board. 1905. Various entrance tests. Stored in the ETS test archives.

Davier, A. A. von, P. W. Holland, and D. T. Thayer. 2004. *The Kernel Method of Test Equating*. New York: Springer-Verlag.

DeMauro. G. E. 1991. The effects of the availability of alternatives and the use of multiple choice or essay anchor tests on constructed response constructs. Draft report. Princeton, NJ: Educational Testing Service.

Dunn, M. C., J. B. Kadane, and J. R. Garrow. 2003. Comparing harm done by mobility and class absence: Missing students and missing data. *Journal of Educational and Behavioral Statistics* 28 (3): 269–288.

Feynman, R. P. 1965. *The Character of Physical Law*. Cambridge: MIT Press.

Finn, C. E., Jr. 1991. *We Must Take Charge: Our Schools and Our Future*. New York: Free Press.

Fitzpatrick, A. R., and W. M. Yen. 1993. The psychometric characteristics of choice items. Paper presented at the Annual Meeting of the National Council on Measurement in Education, April 13, Atlanta.

Fremer, J., R. Jackson, and M. McPeek. 1968. Review of the psychometric characteristics of the Advanced Placement tests in Chemistry, American History, and French. Internal memorandum. Princeton, NJ: Educational Testing Service.

Gelman, A., J. B. Carlin, H. S. Stern, and D. B. Rubin. 1995. *Bayesian Data Analysis*. London: Chapman & Hall.

Gulliksen, H. O. 1950. *A Theory of Mental Tests,* New York: John Wiley & Sons. Reprinted Hillsdale, NJ: Lawrence Erlbaum Associates, 1987.

Haag, C. H. 1985. *Using the PSAT/NMSQT to Help Identify Advanced Placement Students*. Publication 273678. Princeton, NJ: Advanced Placement Program, The College Board.

Hambleton, R. K. 1993. Translating achievement tests for use in cross-national studies. *European Journal of Psychological Assessment* 9:57–68.

Heubert, H., and R. M. Hauser, eds. 1999. *High Stakes: Testing for Tracking, Promotion, and Graduation*. Washington, DC: National Academies Press.

Holland, P. W. 2005. Counterfactuals. In *Encyclopedia of Statistics in Behavioral Science*. Chichester, UK: John Wiley & Sons, 420–422.

Holland, P. W., and D. B. Rubin. 1983. On Lord's paradox. In H. Wainer and S. Messick, eds., *Principals of Modern Psychological Measurement*. Hillsdale, NJ: Lawrence Erlbaum Associates, 3–25.

Hume, D. 1955. *An Inquiry Concerning Human Understanding*. Indianapolis: Bobbs-Merrill.

Jensen, A. R. 1998. *The G Factor: The Science of Mental Ability*. Westport, CT: Praeger.

Kant, I. 1998. *Religion Within the Boundaries of Mere Reason: And Other Writings.* Edited by Robert M. Adams and George Di Giovanni, translated by George Di Giovanni. New York: Cambridge University Press.

Kierkegaard, S. 1986. *Either/Or.* New York: Harper & Row.

Lawrence, I. 1992. *Effect of Calculator Use on SAT-M Score Conversions and Equating*. Draft Report. Princeton, NJ: Educational Testing Service.

Lichten, W., and H. Wainer. 2000. The aptitude-achievement function: An aid for allocating educational resources, with an advanced placement example. *Educational Psychology Review* 12 (2): 201–228.

Little, R.J.A., and D. B. Rubin. 1987. *Statistical Analysis with Missing Data*. New York: Wiley.

Lombard, H. C. 1835. De l'influence des professions sur la durée de la vie. *Annales d'Hygiéne Publique et de Médecine Légale* 14:88–131.

Lord, F. M. 1967. A paradox in the interpretation of group comparisons. *Psychological Bulletin* 68:304–305.

Luce, R. D. 1959. *Individual Choice Behavior*. Wiley: New York.

Lukhele, R., D. Thissen, and H. Wainer. 1994. On the relative value of multiple-choice, constructed response, and examinee-selected items on two achievement tests. *Journal of Educational Measurement* 31:234–250.

Lunz, M. E., and B. A. Bergstrom. 1994. An empirical study of computerized adaptive test administration conditions. *Journal of Educational Measurement* 31:251–263.

Lunz, M. E., B. A. Bergstrom, and B. D. Wright. 1992. The effect of review on student ability and test efficiency for computerized adaptive tests *Applied Psychological Measurement* 16:33–40.

Madden, R. R. 1833. *The Infirmities of Genius, Illustrated by Referring the Anomalies in Literary Character to the Habits and Constitutional Peculiarities of Men of Genius*. London: Saunders and Otley.

Mangel, M., and F. J. Samaniego. 1984. Abraham Wald's work on aircraft survivability. *Journal of the American Statistical Association* 79:259–267.

Massey, D. S., and N. A. Denton. 1993. *American Apartheid: Segregation and the Making of the Underclass*. Cambridge: Harvard University Press.

Mathews, J. 1988. *Escalante: The Best Teacher in America*. New York: Holt.

———. 1998. *Class Struggle*. New York: Times Books.

National Association for College Admission Counseling. 2008 *Report of the Commission on the Use of Standardized Tests in Undergraduate Admission*. Arlington, VA: NACAC. http://www.nacacnet.org/PublicationsResources/Research/Documents/TestingComission_FinalReport.pdf

National Committee on Excellence in Education. 1983. *A Nation at Risk: The Imperative for Educational Reform*. Washington, DC: U.S. Department of Education.

Newrick, P. G., E. Affie, and R.J.M. Corrall. 1990. Relationship between longevity and lifeline: A manual study of 100 patients. *Journal of the Royal Society of Medicine* 83:499–501.

Nieves, E. 1999. Civil rights groups suing Berkeley over admissions policy. *New York Times*, February 3, A1.

Papanastasiou, E. C., and M. D. Reckase. 2007. A "rearrangement procedure" for scoring adaptive tests with review options. *International Journal of Testing* 7:387–407.

Pomplun, M., R. Morgan, and A. Nellikunnel. 1992. *Choice in Advanced Placement Tests.* ETS Statistical Report SR -92-51. Princeton, NJ: Educational Testing Service.

Poortinga, Y. H., and F.J.R. van de Vijver. 1991. Culture-free measurement in the history of cross-cultural psychology. *Bulletin of the International Test Commission* 18:72–87.

Popham, W. J. 1987. The merits of measurement-driven instruction. *Phi delta kappan* 68:679–682.

Powers, D. E., M. E. Fowles, M. Farnum, and K. Gerritz. 1992. *Giving a Choice of Topics on a Test of Basic Writing Skills: Does It Make Any Difference?* Research Report RR 92-19, Princeton, NJ: Educational Testing Service.

Pressley, M., K. Hilden, and R. Shankland. 2002. *An Evaluation of End-Grade-3 Dynamics Indicators of Basic Early Literacy Skills (DIBELS): Speed Reading Without Comprehension.* Technical Report. East Lansing, MI: Literacy Achievement Research Center.

Ravitch, D. 1985. *The Schools We Deserve: Reflections on the Educational Crises of Our Time.* New York: Basic.

Reckase, M. 2004. The real world is more complicated than we would like. *Journal of Educational and Behavioral Statistics* 29 (1): 117–120.

Ree, M. J., and J. A. Earles. 1991a. Predicting training success: Not much more than g. *Personnel Psychology* 44:321–332.

———. 1991b. The stability of convergent estimates of g. *Intelligence* 15:271–278.

———. 1992. Intelligence is the best predictor of job performance. *Current Directions in Psychological Science* 1:86–89.

———. 1993. G is to psychology what carbon is to chemistry: A reply to Sternberg and Wagner, McClelland, and Calfee. *Current Directions in Psychological Science* 2:11–12.

Rosenbaum, P. R. 1995. *Observational Studies.* New York: Springer-Verlag.

———. 2002. *Observational Studies.* 2nd ed. New York: Springer-Verlag.

Rosenfeld, S. 1999. Cal hit with race-bias suit. *San Francisco Examiner*, February 2, A1.

Rubin, D. B., E. A. Stuart, and E. L. Zanutto. 2004. A potential outcomes view of value-added assessment in education. *Journal of Educational and Behavioral Statistics* 29 (1): 103–116.

Salganik, L. H., R. P. Phelps, L. Bianchi, D. Nohara, and T. M. Smith. 1993. *Education in States and Nations: Indicators Comparing U.S. States with the OECD Countries in 1988.* NCES Report No. 93-237. Washington, DC: National Center for Education Statistics.

Sanders, W. L., A. M. Saxton, and S. P. Horn. 1997. The Tennessee Value-Added Educational Assessment System (TVAAS): A quantitative, outcomes-based approach to educational assessment. In J. Millman, ed., *Grading Teachers, Grading Schools: Is Student Achievement a Valid Evaluation Measure?* Thousand Oaks, CA: Corwin Press, 137–162.

Schmidt, W. 2004. The role of content in value-added. Talk presented at the conference Value-Added Modeling: Issues with Theory and Application, University of Maryland, College Park, October 22.

Sireci, S. G. 1997. Problems and issues in linking assessments across languages. *Educational Measurement: Issues and Practice* 16 (1): 12–19, 29.

Sireci, S. G., B. Bastari, and A. Allalouf. 1998. Evaluating construct equivalence across adapted tests. Paper presented at the Annual Meetings of the American Psychological Association, San Francisco, August 14–18.

Thompson, D. W. 1917. *On Growth and Form.* Cambridge: Cambridge University Press.

Thurber, J. 1939. *Fables for Our Time.* New York: Harper & Row.

Tukey, J. W. 1977. *Exploratory Data Analysis.* Reading, MA: Addison-Wesley.

van de Vijver, F.J.R., and Y. H. Poortinga. 1997. Toward an integrated analysis of bias in cross-cultural assessment. *European Journal of Psychological Assessment* 13:29–37.

Vispoel, W. P. 1998. Reviewing and changing answers on computer-adaptive and self-adaptive vocabulary tests. *Journal of Educational Measurement* 35:328–347.

Wainer, H. 1986. *Drawing Inferences from Self-Selected Samples.* New York: Springer-Verlag.

———. 1991. Adjusting for differential base-rates: Lord's paradox again. *Psychological Bulletin* 109:147–151.

———. 1993. Some practical considerations when converting a linearly administered test to an adaptive format. *Educational Measurement: Issues and Practice* 12 (1): 15–20.

———. 1999. The most dangerous profession: A note on nonsampling error. *Psychological Methods* 4 (3): 250–256.

———. 2000. *Computerized Adaptive Testing: A Primer.* 2nd ed. Hillsdale, NJ: Lawrence Erlbaum Associates.

———. 2005. *Graphic Discovery: A Trout in the Milk and Other Visual Adventures.* Princeton, NJ: Princeton University Press.

Wainer, H., and L. Brown. 2004. Two statistical paradoxes in the interpretation of group differences: Illustrated with medical school admission and licensing data. *American Statistician* 58:117–123.

Wainer, H., S. Palmer, and E. T. Bradlow. 1998. A selection of selection anomalies. *Chance* 11 (2): 3–7.

Wainer, H., and L. S. Steinberg. 1992. Sex differences in performance on the mathematics section of the Scholastic Aptitude Test: A bidirectional validity study. *Harvard Educational Review* 62:323–336.

Wainer, H., and D. Thissen. 1993. Combining multiple choice and constructed response test scores: Toward a Marxist theory of test construction. *Applied Measurement in Education* 6:103–118.

———. 1994. On examinee choice in educational testing. *Review of Educational Research* 64:1–40.

Wainer, H., X. Wang, and D. Thissen. 1994. How well can we compare scores on test forms that are constructed by examinees' choice? *Journal of Educational Measurement* 31:183–199.

Wald, A. 1980. A reprint of "A method of estimating plane vulnerability based on damage of survivors." CRC 432, July. http://cna.org/sites/default/files/research/0204320000.pdf.

Wang, X., H. Wainer, and D. Thissen. 1993. On the viability of some untestable assumptions in equating exams that allow examinee choice. *Applied Measurement in Education* 8:211–225.

Willingham, W. W. 1985. *Success in College: The Role of Personal Qualities and Academic Ability.* New York: The College Board.

Willingham, W. W., C. Lewis, R. Morgan, and L. Ramist. 1990. *Predicting College Grades: An Analysis of Institutional Trends over Two Decades.* Princeton, NJ: Educational Testing Service.

Index

achievement tests, 12, 91
  coaching for, 7
  educational resources and, 35, 42, 50
  language and, 25–27
  as optional, xiii, 8–19
  as substitute for aptitude tests, xii, xiv, 20–28, 57, 70
ACT, 9
  coaching for, 7
  elimination of, 7
  as SAT substitute, 15
  value of, 8
admissions exams
  aptitude test substitution and, 20–28
  National Assessment of Educational Progress (NAEP) and, 21
  National Association for College Admission Counseling (NACAC) and, 21–22, 27–31
  optional SAT policy and, xii–xiii, 8–19
  success in predictions of, 20
  value of, 8–19
Admitted Class Evaluation Service (ACES), 9n2
Advanced Placement (AP) program, xiv
  calculus and, 34–51, 55
  chemistry and, 79–81, 84, 105–9
  class size and, 33, 53
  Detroit and, 35, 42–46, 48, 51
  discrimination and, 33
  educational resources allocation and, 32–56
  Escalante and, 35–39, 49n16, 50–51, 54
  examinee choice and, 79–81, 84, 99
  Garfield High School and, 35–45, 49n16, 51, 54
  generalizations for, 46–50
  La Cañada High School and, 35, 39–46
  language and, 49n16, 51–52, 55–56
  national projection and, 50–51
  placement error and, 55

  popularity of, 33
  PSAT and, 32–56
  recruitment and, 36–44
  SAT and, 32–33, 36–37, 42–43, 51–53
  Spanish and, 49n16, 51
  state support of, 33
  stereotypes and, 36
  student potential and, 51
  subject content and, 32
  U.S. history test of 1988 and, 80–82
Affie, E., 145n6
Aiken, Howard, 155
Alexander the Great, 3
Ali, Muhammad, 22n2
Allalouf, Avi, 57n1, 68n7
American Society of Podiatry, 145
anchor items, 58–61, 64–67, 70
Angoff, W. H., 63, 68n7
Arabic, 65–66
Aristotle, 2–3
'αρμονια, 108n8
armor, 131–34
Army Alpha tests, 6
Avery, Christopher, 139, 141n2, 142

Bacon, Francis, 3
Baldwin, Peter, xii
Ballou, D., 121n2
barroom brawls, 145
Bastari, B., 68n7
Bayesian theory, 69
Beast, number of, 666
Beaton, Albert, 134
"Bell Curve, The" (Gawande), 140
Beller, Michal, 65n6, 68–69
Berkeley, George, 3
Betamax, 8
bias
  examinee choice and, 79, 84, 87
  statistics and, 132–34, 141–43, 146
  tests and, 20–21, 54, 67–68